COOK'S
MARKETPLACE
CHICAGO

OTHER BOOKS IN COOK'S MARKETPLACE SERIES

COOK'S
MARKETPLACE

CHICAGO

Carol Haddix & Sherman Kaplan

101 Productions • San Francisco

Printed and bound in the United States of America.

Distributed to the book trade in the United States
by the Macmillan Publishing Company, New York.

Published by 101 Productions
834 Mission Street
San Francisco, California 94103

Library of Congress Cataloging-in-Publication Data

Kaplan, Sherman, 1941–
    Cook's marketplace Chicago.

    Includes index.
    1. Marketing (Home economics)—Illinois—Chicago—
Directories. 2. Grocery trade—Illinois—Chicago—
Directories. 3. Kitchen utensils—Illinois—Chicago
Directories. 4. Cooking schools—Illinois—Chicago—
Directories. I. Haddix, Carol. II. Title.
TX356.K37   1986   381'.45641'0977311   86-2441
ISBN 0-89286-251-3

Contents

Introduction

Searching out the Chicago area's ethnic markets, gourmet specialty stores, cookware shops, cooking classes and the like becomes an education in more than culinary matters. The field is as diverse as the city and its neighborhoods, because Chicago is as much a cooking pot, as it is a melting pot. In the course of researching *Cook's Marketplace Chicago*, we learned more than we expected about the people of our city, how they live and how they eat. Within the city and its suburbs, an area of 228 square miles, we found virtually every kind of prepared ethnic food we could want, as well as the ingredients to make those foods. While there is a tremendous interest in cooking here, there are also many Chicagoans who appreciate good food, but do not have the time to prepare it.

We approached the writing of *Cook's Marketplace Chicago* from two separate directions. Carol, who is food editor for *The Chicago Tribune*, undertook her search as an experienced cook, who not only knows her way around Chicago, but around a kitchen. Sherman, a news anchor and reporter for WBBM-AM, the CBS all-news radio station, has reviewed restaurants in the city for some seventeen years, and looked at the *Cook's Marketplace* project from the consumer's viewpoint. So, our book is the collaboration of a dedicated cook and a confirmed eater.

Our intent in writing *Cook's Marketplace Chicago* has not been to do a "best of . . ." kind of guide. Instead, we wanted to show how diverse Chicago shopping can be beyond the standard, neighborhood chain supermarket. Undoubtedly, you will find some of your favorite shops. We hope you will also discover, as have we, the quaint, the hidden, the unusual. We'll lead you to sources for tahini, saffron, plantains. We'll show you where to find a boutique winery, as well as shops that stock the wines of the world. We'll take you into sausage shops where you'll find links that taste the way they did in Old World Hungary, Russia, Germany, Poland or Italy. We'll share with you sources for bulk grains, herbs and spices, nuts from the bin. We'll show you where to buy coffee freshly roasted or leaf teas tnat nave never seen the inside of a bag.

When using this book, please do not look on shopping as a chore. Think of it as recreation. Prowl Devon Avenue and savor the ethnic diversities that range from Eastern European to Indian. Walk through Chinatown where The New Quan Wah has whole roasted ducks hanging by their feet in the front window. Visit Ganache in Evanston, where it almost seems you can put on weight just by looking at the riches of their cakes, brownies and luscious pastries. And for those times when you do not want to do the cooking yourself, visit Mitchell Cobey's for fine prepared curried chicken salad or ratatouille.

Cook's Marketplace Chicago is organized by foods, services and supplies. In some cases, we have subdivided our chapters beyond the main headings. Listings are alphabetized; under Ethnic Foods, for example, you'll find shops listed under Latin, Chinese, Japanese, Thai, Middle Eastern, Italian, German, and so forth. All entries are cross-indexed as well. We have listed hours for all the stores, but many do change so we suggest you call ahead before visiting.

If we had included every ethnic market, cookware store and specialty shop, this book would be the size of The Yellow Pages. Consider our guide a starting point. If you find a source not listed here, and care to share it with us for a future edition of *Cook's Marketplace Chicago*, please write to us in care of our publisher, 101 Productions, 834 Mission Street, San Francisco, California 94103.

Finally, we must thank all of those people who offered their suggestions, help and information. Foremost among them are Maria Battaglia, JeanMarie Brownson, Carolyn Buster, Elaine Sherman, Pat Tennison and Camille Stagg.

COOK'S
MARKETPLACE
CHICAGO

Baked Goods

Chicago might not be known for fine pastry shops. (The city still relies on its Wonder Bread, Sara Lee and Keebler bakery/factories.) Yet, when you explore the neighborhoods, it's easy to find old-time bakeries that specialize in goods like babka, hearty German rye breads and Austrian whipped-cream tortes which are of good quality and reasonably priced.

Again, as in the case of many other foodstuffs, the city's wide diversity of ethnic populations creates our interesting bakeries. Rather than the fine, elegant pastries of France, you'll find hearty sour cream coffeecakes and towering American carrot cakes and breads of Eastern Europe. While glitzier pastry shops come and go, the neighborhoods form the backbone of Chicago's small baking industry.

In addition to the establishments that follow, mention also must be made of Marshall Field's bakery, noted for its Frango mint brownies, fudgy concoctions that are even more delicious than Field's famous Frango candies. The in-store bakery also supplies fine breads, cakes and cookies. Neiman-Marcus also has a good supply of baked goods gathered from local sources, including Boudin sourdough breads.

In addition to Marshall Field and Neiman-Marcus other stores listed in the chapter on Gourmet & Takeout Foods have good bakery sections. See An Apple a Day, Foodstuffs, Foodworks, Hel's Kitchen, Kenessy's, LaBelle Gourmet, and Zambrana's. Many of the shops in Ethnic Foods also carry baked goods, such as the Middle Eastern Bakery and, for Chinese, the Phoenix Company Bakery. Also see the Bread Shop in the Health Foods chapter.

American

AUGUSTA BAKERY CORP.
901 North Ashland Avenue, Chicago 60622. Telephone 486-1017 or 486-1018.
Hours: M–SAT 6–6:30, SUN 6–1.

Known for its fine rye breads, this wholesale and retail bakery serves many of the city's fine food shops and restaurants. Despite its out-of-the-way location west of the Loop, the shop still draws customers from all over the city and suburbs. A full line of pies, cakes and cookies also is available. Go early in the morning, though, for the best selection.

BOUDIN SOUR DOUGH BAKERY
63 East Chicago Avenue, Chicago 60610. Telephone 329-1580. Hours: M–TH
7–7, F 7–10, SAT 9–10, SUN 10–5.
31 Old Orchard Shopping Center, Skokie 60076. Telephone 677-0093.
Hours: M–F 8–9, SAT–SUN 8–5:30.

The famous San Francisco sourdough bread has successfully made the transition to the Midwest and Chicagoans appear thankful, indeed. The loaves of tangy bread are beautiful and full of flavor, especially the rye. There's nothing better than a sandwich made with thick slices or rolls of sourdough. You can order from a small selection of sandwiches in the shops and sit down to enjoy a taste of San Francisco.

CHEESECAKES BY JR
2841 West Howard Street, Chicago 60645. Telephone 465-6733. Hours: M–F
9–8, SAT 9–6.

Janet Rosing went into the retail business a few years back after friends raved about her homemade cheesecakes. Today her small bakery has a small unassuming front sales area with one small refrigerated case that holds the cheesecakes for the day. Her strawberry cheesecake captures the fresh flavor of the strawberries nestled inside the cake as well as in the topping. Others flavors recently offered include chocolate, chocolate chip and blueberry. The owner also supplies restaurants and gourmet shops in town and bakes special cakes, including stunning wedding cheesecakes.

LE CHEESECAKE
3150 Skokie Valley Road, Highland Park 60035. Telephone 432-4700. Hours: M–SAT 9–5.

A favorite family recipe spawned this small carry-out business. At last count, Le Cheesecake provided eleven different flavors of cheesecake. They include some unusual choices such as piña colada, chocolate chip, pumpkin and peanut butter, just to name a few. Cakes are sold in full twelve-inch diameter rounds or in half sizes, with prices pegged to the cost of ingredients.

CHICAGO BAKING CO.
1003 West Armitage Street, Chicago 60614. Telephone 549-5800. Hours M–F 6:30–6:30, SAT 7–5:30, SUN 8–3.

This tiny bakery makes decent Italian-style and French breads in baguettes, short or round loaves and rolls. A crisp crust encloses a nice chewy and yeasty crumb. Many of the city's restaurants use the bakery's baguettes as their house bread. A small line of cookies is also available.

COOKIEMANIA
3145 North Halsted, Chicago 60657. Telephone 935-5566. Hours: M–SAT 8–4:30.

Jeri Dry and Alix Engel bill their products as "The world's most expensive cookies." After baking Christmas cookies yearly for friends and neighbors, the women decided to put their talent to the monetary test in 1981, resulting in one of Chicago's most successful business stories. Now Cookiemania cookies are sold in department stores nationwide and under the private labels of Saks Fifth Avenue and Bloomingdale's. But the cookies are still made by hand in ten varieties at the rate of about six thousand pounds a week. Most of the all-butter cookies come in an attractive red tin and are sold by mail order. Boxes and individual large cookies also are available at the store. The owners proudly tell the tale of another successful cookie entrepreneur, Famous Amos, who stopped by the store and proclaimed Cookiemania's mini chocolate chip cookies second best in the United States—second only to his, of course.

FRESH START BAKERY
3002 North Sheffield Avenue, Chicago 60657. Telephone 348-8500. Hours: 6:30–6 daily.

Good, old-fashioned American desserts can be found at this small North Side wholesale bakery and catering shop run by a group of young pastry cooks. Great champagne cheesecake, apple Bavarian torte, chocolate cakes and macadamia nut tart are all fresh and very tempting. Call a day ahead to order whole cakes. Some prepared foods to go are also offered.

LET THEM EAT CAKE
948 North Rush Street, Chicago 60610. Hours: M–TH 8–8, F–SAT 8–midnight.
1701 West Foster Avenue, Chicago 60640. Hours: M–SAT 8–6.
3339 Dempster Avenue, Skokie. Hours: M–SAT 9–6.
Central order telephone: 728-4040.

Known for its special-occasion cakes, this bakery chain offers a full line of pastries, cookies and cakes. Custom decorated cakes come in such amusing forms as hamburgers, pizzas, pinball games, human shapes and even computers.

Caribbean

CARIBBEAN AMERICAN BAKING COMPANY
1551 West Howard Street, Chicago 60626. Telephone 761-0700. Hours: M–SAT 8–10, SUN noon–9.

One of the most unusual of the city's bakeries, this is perhaps the only place in Chicago to offer Jamaican baked goods. Good quality, intriguing items include beef patties, or turnovers, filled with a curried ground beef mixture; spiced bun, a loaf of sweet bread filled with raisins, citrus peel and cherries; coconut bread; gingerbread; and plantain tarts. A nicely textured whole-wheat bread is also offered. The beef patties make excellent hors d'oeuvre. Try them with a cold Mexican beer or, if you can find one, a Jamaican brew.

Chinese

GARDEN BAKERY
237 West Cermak Road, Chicago 60616. Telephone 225-1999. Hours: F–W 9–8.

In the mood for deep-fried taro? Well, even if you aren't, this is just one of the fine bakeries in Chinatown that is worth a stop, if for nothing else than to try a nibble of such exotics. For the timid palate, the custard tarts and filled buns are more to non-Oriental tastes. The bakery will produce party trays with advance notice. Ask for Sam.

GARDEN BAKERY
2358 South Wentworth Avenue, Chicago 60616. Telephone 225-2730. Hours: W–M 9–7.

Nestled near one end of Chinatown's main street, this small bakery serves forth some intriguing Chinese sweet pastries such as large custard tarts and buns filled with bean paste, sausage, chicken or egg and ham. The fine barbecued pork-filled buns alone are worth the trip. The almond cookies are also tops—no comparison to those you find in many Chinese restaurants and the prices are very reasonable.

KEEFER BAKERY INC.
249 West Cermak Road, Chicago 60616. Telephone 326-2289. Hours: M–F
9–6:30, SAT–SUN 9–7.
Despite the non-Oriental name, this small shop in Chinatown offers the traditional Oriental barbecue buns, lotus cakes and excellent custard buns.

European

ALBERT'S CAFE & PATISSERIE
52 West Elm Street, Chicago 60610. Telephone 751-0666. Hours: TU–F
10–9:30, SAT 9–9:30, SUN 10–9.
One of the few bakeries in Chicago that's reminiscent of European patisseries, this gleaming little spot makes daily a small selection of tortes, cheesecakes, beautifully formed cookies, croissants and breads. Chef Albert Wolf also prepares a small menu of sandwiches, pâtés, quiches and salads for the inexpensive twenty-eight-seat cafe. In summer, outdoor tables provide an ideal way to enjoy a morning espresso and croissants, French-style.

CAFE BENNISON
1183 Wilmette Avenue, Wilmette 60091. Telephone 251-0194; Hours: 7–6
M–SAT. Ask to be placed on mailing list.
This is about as close to a Viennese pastry shop as you will find on the North Shore. Assorted tortes, cakes, pies and breads crowd the cases and shelves. And often there are pastry-wrapped entrees for carry-out such as a salmon coulibiac or beef Wellington. The takeout fare also includes individual tart-sized quiches, soups, fresh pâtés, brioches, croissants and picnic baskets which are especially popular during the summertime Ravinia Festival season.

CAFE SELMARIE
Lincoln Square Shopping Mall, 2327 West Giddings, Chicago 60625. Telephone
989-5595. Hours: TU–TH 10–8, F–SAT 10–10, SUN 10–8.
This two-year-old combination cafe and bakery specializes in fresh fruit and whipped cream tortes such as black forest, linzer and butter cakes. Also made on the premises are cookies, muffins, strudel, truffles and fruit tarts, as well as quiches, soups and sandwiches. The bakery was started by two neighborhood women who use only fresh ingredients and none of those "standard bakery fillings." It's like a taste of Europe when you dig into a generous slice of torte or delicious apple butter cake and sip on espresso at one of the five tiny tables. The cafe is hard to find, located on a concourse off a small shopping mall in this northwest area where many German-American families have settled.

DEBORAH'S COUNTRY FRENCH BREAD
500 North Orleans Street, Chicago 60610. Telephone 321-6021. Mail order only.

The idea of this enterprise may seem silly, but apparently it's working. Food aficionados who travel to France often make a point to visit the famous Poulaine bakery and sample the hearty, country-style loaves baked in old wood-burning ovens. Deborah conceived the idea that Chicagoans might like to try the french bread in their own hometown and pulled a coup by being the first to air ship here loaves of frozen Poulaine bread. She sells it only by mail in gift boxes for a whopping $25 per loaf. But is this admittedly fine bread worth $25? That's the question.

FOREST VIEW BAKERY
6454 North Milwaukee Avenue, Chicago 60631. Telephone 631-1129. Hours:
M–SAT 6–6, SUN 7–2.

Opposite a forest preserve on the northwest edge of Chicago, this small, typical bakery specializes in fine Polish baked goods including babkas, mazureks, cheesecakes and bismarks at reasonable prices.

GANACHE
1511 Sherman Avenue, Evanston 60201. Telephone 864-4424. Hours: TU–SAT
10–6.

This handsome new pastry shop in an Evanston landmark building is an elegant little store offering box lunches and desserts. The repertoire ranges from a mini devils food cake for two to a sumptuous marjolaine. Box lunches include sandwiches on fresh baked bread, light salads, muffins and brownies. Party desserts range from French chocolate tortes and fancy whipped cream cakes to cheesecakes, fruit tarts and gift-boxed chocolate truffles. Ganache features parking next door, deliveries, phone orders and gift baskets. The idea is convenience in all its forms.

HOEFFKEN'S, THE BUSY BAKERY
3044 West 63rd Street, Chicago 60629. Telephone 737-0390. Hours: M–F 6–5:30, SAT 6–5.

And busy it is on a Saturday morning. Although Hoeffken is an Irish name, few Irish baked goods, other than soda bread, are sold in this forty-year-old shop. Instead, a loyal following lines up for rainbow whipped-cream cakes, fruit pies and houska, a chewy, twisted egg bread.

LUTZ CONTINENTAL PASTRIES & CANDIES
2458 West Montrose Avenue, Chicago 60618. Telephone 478-7785. Hours: TU–SUN 7–10.

One of the most popular bakeries in Chicago since the 1950s, Lutz has earned a reputation beyond the city, too. Out-of-town visitors come to this North Side neighborhood to pick up fancy boxes of marzipan and candies (especially at holidays when the boxes are beautifully decorated) and to buy the hearty German breads and Viennese tortes. In the back of the bakery, a small cafe serves European lunches and light dinners that only end properly, of course, with a generous slice of gooseberry or fresh strawberry whipped-cream torte or any of a long list of desserts. The strong coffee comes *mit schlag*, a pitcherful of unsweetened whipped cream. It's caloric heaven.

MAISON BARUSSEAU
592 Roger Williams Avenue, Highland Park 60035. Telephone 432-1033. Hours: TU–SAT 7:30–7, SUN 8–2.

This small storefront shop in Highland Park's Ravinia neighborhood turns out a consistently excellent selection of fresh products. Chef Guy Barusseau has four decades of experience as a French baker, using old-fashioned methods whether he's making croissants or gâteaux, quiches or bouchées. In addition to the regular inventory of baked goods and a variety of fruit tarts, the shop serves up seasonal specials such as a bûche de Noël for Christmas. Luncheon soups and sandwiches are also available for carry-out or enjoying at one of the small cafe tables. Gnocchi à la Parisienne, onion soup and spinach tart are among the choices.

MIARA'S CONTINENTAL PASTRY
7053 West Addison Street, Chicago 60634. Telephone 725-3818. Hours: TU–SAT 6–6, SUN 7–1:30.

Luscious displays in the European style make it impossible to resist buying more than you need at this West Side pastry shop. In addition to German kuchens, Viennese strudels, French fruit tarts, Polish cheese breads and Italian cannoli, the shop owners make their own truffles and other candies with imported chocolate and display them in an eye-catching revolving circular glass case.

ROLF'S PATISSERIE
3304 North Broadway Avenue, Chicago 60657. Telephone 477-6300. Hours: TU–F 8:30–9, SAT 8:30–7, SUN 8:30–5.

Fine-looking cheesecakes, chocolate cakes, tortes and cookies line the cases in this small, attractive shop on the North Side. A few tables allow browsers to sample before they buy or simply enjoy coffee and cake. A must is the apple cake, a moist, butter cake topped with apples and cinnamon—a perfectly decadent way to start breakfast.

THE UPPER CRUST
2737 Pfingsten Road (at Willow), Glenview 60025. Telephone 564-2285. Hours: M–SAT 9–7, SUN 9–2.

As the saying goes, build a better mousetrap. Well, the same thing can be said about breads. The Upper Crust is the next best thing to having your own custom baker. While most commercial bakeries bake overnight, The Upper Crust is baking all day long. Almost anytime you walk in, someone will be popping something in, or hauling something out of an oven. These are not just ordinary loaf breads, either. The store features gourmet European specialty breads made with no sugar, no salt, no preservatives and no additives. Although special orders require a day's advance notice, most any time you can walk in and get a five-grain bread, or brioche or high-fiber bran from among the several choices. This all-day baking is a neat and new idea that's likely to be a big hit among food shoppers who want the quality only freshness can bring, but do not have the time to bake.

URBAUER BAKERY
1414 West 51st Street, Chicago 60609. Telephone 927-5550. Hours: TH–SAT 6–5.

This tiny bakery dates back fifty years in a neighborhood that has seen many changes. The Austrian poppyseed and walnut strudels don't sell as well to the new Latin neighbors, but these pastries are worth a trip. Also try the crispy salt sticks.

VIENNA PASTRY SHOP
5411 West Addison, Chicago 60641. Telephone 685-4166. Hours: TU–SAT 7–6, SUN 8–1.

Gerhard Kaes and his wife Hedwig arrived in America from Vienna in 1964 and opened shop two years later in this mainly residential neighborhood. Gerhard's family had been in the baking business for three generations and the pastry chef has continued his family's reputation with fine strudels and kolachky, plus some two dozen tortes including the dobos and linzer varieties. The spick-and-span bakery is now run with the help of the Kaes children.

German

HUNSSINGER'S BAKERY
2410 West 111th Street, Chicago 60655. Telephone 445-5909. Hours: M–F 6–6, SAT 6–5:30.

This German bakery produces a great, mild rye bread that helps create long lines on a busy Saturday morning. Also worth buying are the potato and limpa breads and a sign on the door suggests customers try the whipped-cream cakes, another specialty. Friendly service and a neighborhood feel make this spot worth a stop if you're on the southwest side.

Greek

PAN HELLENIC PASTRY SHOP
322 South Halsted Street, Chicago, 60606. Telephone 454-1886. Hours: M–TH 9–8, F–SAT 9–11, SUN 12–8.

Louis and Helen Manolakos run a bakery that's a must stop during a trip to Chicago's old Greektown just west of the Loop. Louis is proud of his baklava, both his traditional recipe and the special baklava of his own creation with a touch of cinnamon and raisins in the filling. His phyllo-wrapped spinach and cheese turnovers are a hefty lunch and you can sit and eat them with a cup of Greek coffee at one of two tables. Cookies, custard-filled phyllo rectangles and other Greek specialties make it difficult to choose just one item.

Italian

BALICE BAKERY/CALABRESE BAKING COMPANY
7639 West Belmont, Elmwood Park, 60635. Hours: TU–SAT 8–6, SUN 8–1.
Crispy Italian breads are the specialty in this family-run bakery in one of Chicago's west suburban Italian neighborhoods. The bread can also be found in many of the city's Italian eateries. Whole-wheat breads, freselle, packaged thick-crust pizza, cannoli, svogliatelle, pasticciotti and assorted cookies line the cases.

D'AMATO'S ITALIAN & FRENCH BAKERY
1124 West Grand Avenue, Chicago 60622. Telephone 733-5456. Hours: TU–F 8–6:30, SAT 8–5:30, SUN 8–1:30.
Dine in Chicago's fine Italian restaurants and you'll probably get a basket of D'Amato's bread before your meal. It's crisp on the outside, thanks to the old wood-burning oven it is baked in (one of only a handful of wood-burning bread ovens in town), and chewy and yeasty on the inside. The bread comes in one- or two-pound round or rectangular loaves and in buns. It also serves as the sensational crust in sausage or cheese pan pizzas and the staff will warm up the pizza for you in case you can't wait until you get home to eat it. It's no wonder D'Amato's has been called the best Italian bakery in town by food experts. Owner Nick D'Amato and sons also make fine French baguettes.

ORIGINAL FERRARRA
2210 West Taylor, Chicago 60612. Telephone 666-2200. Hours: M–SAT 8:30–5, SUN 8:30–1.
One of Chicago's oldest Italian bakeries, Original Ferrarra was founded in 1908 at the corner of Halsted and Taylor in what was once the heart of Chicago's Italian community. But the bakery moved further west in the 1960s to make way for the University of Illinois' Chicago campus. Specializing in traditional Italian pastries such as cannoli and cookies, the shop serves the remaining Italian customers in this old neighborhood. Wedding cakes are a specialty. No breads are made here.

SCAFURI BAKERY
1337 West Taylor Street, Chicago 60607. Telephone 733-8881. Hours: TU–SAT 7–5, SUN 7–1.
The neighborhood kids come in for the great rectangular pans of cheese or sausage pizza in this tiny bakery that has been serving the Italian community for seventy-five years. The daughter of the original owner now runs the place. Italian cookies, pastries, some pies and crispy-crusted loaves of Italian bread and bread sticks are also good.

Swedish

SWEDISH BAKERY
5348 North Clark Street, Chicago 60640. Telephone 561-8919. Hours: TU–F 7–6, SAT 7–5:30.

Smack in the middle of Andersonville, Chicago's Swedish neighborhood, lies this family-owned bakery which specializes in pastries such as marzipan cakes, fruit tortes, cardamom coffeecakes and the strange pastries called toskas, which look like two hamburger buns stuck together with a thick layer of filling. They're not really sweet and could almost be a breakfast cake. A nice assortment of Swedish butter cookies is also displayed.

SWEDISH CAFE AND PASTRY MAKER
3258 West Foster Avenue, Chicago 60625. Telephone 588-7402. Hours: TU–F 10–5:30, SAT 10–5.

Here's a recently opened and charming little cafe, decorated in blue and white with lace curtains, six blue-clothed tables and an array of enticing baked goods. You'll find Swedish limpa bread, that anise and orange-flavored loaf, pumpernickel, an assortment of coffeecakes filled with fruit and tortes made with lemon coconut or hazelnut and a Danish layer torte filled with raspberry jam. Sandwiches include a simple ham salad or crab and shrimp salad on croissants or pumpernickel. If the weather is good and you don't want to sit inside, take your goodies across the street to the North Park College green and have a picnic.

Chocolate & Sweets

Man's sweet tooth is virtually universal, but the taste for chocolate is a gift of the New World. Cortez may have been the first European to bring "chocolatl" eastward across the Atlantic as a consequence of his encounter with the Aztecs. Chocolate soon became a favorite among the Spanish aristocracy, but it took another hundred years before the secrets of this exotic drink began spreading through the rest of Europe. Just as they would in coffeehouses, people would gather to sip chocolate drinks.

The French produced the first chocolate candy bars, adding a new dimension to the way people could savor the complex flavors of the cocoa bean. Later, the Swiss added milk to the product, creating a new variety that ultimately was to become the most popular form of chocolate.

Most of the following listings are sources for cooking chocolates, as well as better candies. The literature on chocolate has become vast in recent years, as our tastes have grown for better, richer, and more deeply flavored chocolates. We have also included sources for other candies of interest to the gourmand such as toffees, caramels and some intense fruit-flavored sweets.

For more exotic alternatives to the standard hard candies, check such sources as the Indian and Middle Eastern groceries in the chapter on Ethnic Foods. Many bakeries and pastry shops also carry lines of chocolate products; be sure to check the listings, such as Miara's Continental Pastry, under Baked Goods. Among the shops in the Gourmet & Takeout Foods section with good candy selections are Marshall Field, Foodstuff and Neiman-Marcus.

CORA LEE CANDIES
995 Waukegan Road, Glenview 60015. Telephone 724-2754. Hours: M–SAT 9–6.
   If you did a blind taste test of toffees, Cora Lee Candies would win against most any challenger. This small shop, in the same spot for some thirty-five years, is a favorite for demanding shoppers who need a special candy. The store makes its own toffees and chocolates in the back, as well as specially designed candies for birthdays, graduations and holidays. The store has that wonderful aroma of a candy shop and it's a pleasure just to walk in, even if you don't need anything. But, chances are you won't want to leave without a smidge of that toffee!

CUNIS CANDIES
1030 East 162nd, South Holland, Indiana 60473. Telephone 596-2440. Hours: M–SAT 11–11.
   This nondescript shop in a suburban shopping center serves up some of the best hand-dipped candies and rich ice creams in the Chicago area. The ice cream contains no preservatives and is made with only natural fruit flavors, including peach and blueberry in season. A full line of soda fountain favorites, including a dynamite hot fudge sundae, is available to savor in the Formica booths. The shop specializes in molded chocolates for holidays.

FANNY MAY KITCHEN FRESH CANDY SHOPS
Headquarters: 1137 West Jackson Boulevard, Chicago 60607. Telephone 243-2700. Many locations with varied hours.
   Fanny May is a Chicago institution, with a store on practically every corner. It is a source of medium-priced chocolates, mints and nut candies at about thirty stores throughout the Chicago area.

GODIVA

Water Tower Place, 845 North Michigan Avenue, Chicago 60610. Telephone 280-1133. Hours: TU, W, F, SAT 10–6:30; M, TH 10–7:30; SUN noon–5.

This gleaming gem of a shop is as irresistible to tourists in Water Tower Place as Mrs. Field's cookie shop next door. Godiva specializes in gift boxes of well-known, American-made chocolates, including a stunning shell-shaped collection.

HUWYLER'S

535 North Michigan Avenue, Chicago 60611. Telephone 923-0028. Hours: M–SAT 10–6. Mailing list.

Many of Huwyler's chocolates, including assorted truffles and pralines, are made by hand in Switzerland and flown into Chicago weekly. The company never refrigerates nor freezes their chocolates. Huwylers also makes candies on the premises, using only natural ingredients, without chemical preservatives. While strolling along Michigan Avenue, you might want to stop and tease your tastebuds by watching one of the chocolatiers right in the front window dipping fresh fruits into the kettles of warm, creamy dark or white chocolate. Out come coated banana chunks or juicy long stem cherries, even raspberries or blackberries. In addition to the hand-dipped and other prepared chocolates, the shop offers a few cakes and tortes. You can enjoy a slice at a small table in the store, along with a cup of coffee or cocoa, or take home a larger purchase for yourself, or perhaps as a gift.

IDEAL CANDY SHOP

3311 North Clark Street, Chicago 60657. Telephone 327-2880. Hours: W–SAT 11–9:30, SUN 11–5.

A neighborhood shop that specializes in all kinds of chocolates, homemade fudge and caramel candies made on the premises.

KRON CHOCOLATIER

Water Tower Place, 835 North Michigan Avenue, Chicago 60610. Telephone 943-8444. Hours: M–TH 8–9:30, F–SAT 8–midnight, SUN 8:30–9:30.

Kron specializes in custom-made molded chocolate in such shapes as tennis rackets, human figures or numbers and letters.

LONG GROVE CONFECTIONARY
Main store: 220 Coffin Road, Long Grove 60047. Telephone 634-9000.
Drake Hotel, 140 East Walton Street, Chicago 60611. Telephone 642-1684.
Plaza del Lago, 1515 Sheridan Road, Wilmette 60091. Telephone 251-7400.
Carillon Square, 1450 Waukegan Road, Glenview 60015. Telephone 729-1113.
All stores open daily; hours vary. Telephone orders 634-9001. Ask to be placed
on free mailing list.

Fine handmade chocolates are featured here, as well as specialty molds using only premium ingredients such as ninety-three score butter, whipping cream, pure vanilla and freshly roasted nuts. In the main store you can see the candies being made in a glassed-in preparation area. The confectionary now offers over a hundred versions of chocolate and chocolate specialty items, including chocolate container molds that can be used for your own creations. Other popular candies here include English toffee, almond bark, honey-glazed fruits dipped in chocolate, nut clusters of cashews, pistachios or macadamias, plus butter creams and truffles.

MADAME CHOCOLATE
1940-C Lehigh Avenue, Glenview 60025. Telephone 729-3330. Hours: M–F
12–4. An excellent catalog is published three times a year and is available by
request. The catalog alone is an education about chocolates.

For a while, it looked as if the only thing Elaine Sherman might have to sell would be burnt chocolate. A fire in the building which houses Madame Chocolate just about did in the business. But, like the proverbial phoenix that rose from the ashes, so too has Madame Chocolate. This may be the only retail outlet in the nation to stock such a complete line of high-quality European and domestic chocolates for the cook, baker, candymaker, amateur, professional and just plain chocoholic. Lines stocked include widely known brands such as Lindt, Ghirardelli and Callebaut, as well as boutique chocolates from small specialty producers. You will find unsweetened, bittersweet, semisweet and white chocolates, sauces, cocoa, bits, chips and chunks, not to mention all the tools needed for successful cooking with chocolate. The store is really little more than a warehouse since the bulk of business is done by mail order or phone and shipped to any destination you select. But, visitors are always welcome and Madame Chocolate herself will usually be there to conduct a taste tour of her inventory and answer any questions you may have about storage, handling and cooking with chocolate.

MARGIE'S CANDIES
1960 North Western Avenue, Chicago 60647. Telephone 384-1035. Hours:
M–TH 9–midnight, F–SAT 9–1 a.m.

An old-fashioned candy store, complete with toys, stuffed animals, and gift baskets lining the shelves. Good-quality, medium priced candies.

MARTHA'S CANDY SHOP
3257 North Broadway Avenue, Chicago 60657. Telephone 248-8733. Hours: M–SAT 9–7, SUN 11–4.

A spic-and-span fifty-five-year-old shop on a busy street in the Uptown area, Martha's has consistently turned out quality chocolate candy made from a high-grade American chocolate. Creams, nut clusters, caramels and a whole line of filled chocolates are weighed out by a friendly staff.

MARSHALL FIELD & CO.
111 North State Street, Chicago 60602. Candy department. Telephone 781-4656. Hours: TU, W, F, SAT 9:45–5:45; M, TH 9:45–7.

Field's has its own candy kitchen in the State Street store where good quality chocolates, including the famous Frango mints, are prepared. The mints are small rectangles of pure chocolate flavored with a refreshing mint that is not overpowering like so many mint candies. Frangos also come in other assorted flavors such as raspberry, orange and, a personal favorite, peanut butter. Imported chocolates such as Töbler, Lindt and Michel Guérard also are stocked in what has to be the city's most extensive candy department.

THORNTON'S ENGLISH CHOCOLATE SHOP
Water Tower Place, 845 North Michigan Avenue, Chicago 60610. Telephone 266-3415. Hours: M, TH 10–7; T, W, F, SAT 10–6; SUN noon–5.

English-style chocolates here include creams, nuts and truffles in many flavors. But the best things in this quaint shop, located in Water Tower Place, are the several flavors of toffee, including a fine Brazil nut and a pecan treacle. Great-looking bags and boxes are available for gift packaging.

UNIVERSAL CANDIES
3056 South Ashland Avenue, Chicago 60609. Telephone 778-9580 or 383-0988. Hours: 9–9:30 daily.

Candies are made on the premises just the way they've been made for forty-three years. Owners Chester and James Laciak specialize in wholesale and retail chocolates, including nut clusters and delicious pecan yum yums (caramel, pecans and chocolate). Orange peels and coconut clusters are also big sellers. Ice cream, sodas and malts supplement the candy selection, especially in the summer. Let's hope this and other family-run candy shops can stay in business in the face of all the glitzy, national candy companies showing up in town.

Coffee & Tea

As legend has it, the stimulant effects of coffee were first noted centuries ago by a young goatherd on the Arabian Peninsula who wondered why one of his goats became so frisky after nibbling on a certain berry. Then the boy tasted the berries from the same bush, and, well, the rest is history.

Whatever its origins, man's insatiable taste for coffee has been unabated until the present time. True, we may not have the hundreds of coffeehouses that dotted Samuel Johnson's London, but we can't overlook the number of specialty shops in and around Chicago that trade solely in coffees, teas and the equipment with which to brew and serve them properly.

Virtually all of the small shops listed here have a wide choice of fresh coffee beans on hand. Many will have their own recommended house blends. Teas represent a broad spectrum of the Orient. Most shops will be happy to supply you with full information on the best way to store, brew and serve coffees and teas. As a general practice, keep your beans in an air-tight bag in the freezer until just before you grind them. Similarly, if the shop grinds the beans at time of purchase, keep the grind frozen until you are ready to brew. In the latter case, it is best to use your ground coffee within a month or two at the most. Whole beans, when properly stored, will keep longer.

Tea should not be kept frozen, but it should be stored in a dry place so that the leaves will not deteriorate from humidity. When brewing either beverage, try to use a bottled or filtered water from which all chemicals have been removed. You'll get a much more satisfying brew in the bargain.

Tea should be allowed to steep in not quite boiling water for three to five minutes, depending upon how strong you like it. Most coffee lovers swear by their drip pots, claiming that percolating actually boils the coffee, rather than brews it. As for decaffeinated coffees, treat them the same as you would regular. Incidentally, virtually all the shops listed in *Cook's Marketplace Chicago* sell water-processed, instead of chemically processed decaffeinated coffee.

In addition to the listings that follow, look for coffee at Gold Standard Liquors and the Chalet Wine and Cheese shops in the Wines chapter. Also check Convito Italiano and other Italian shops listed in Ethnic Foods, as well as Foodstuffs ana Foodworks in Gourmet & Takeout Foods. Other sources for coffee include Marshall Field, Treasure Island, Neiman-Marcus, Zambranas and La Salle Street Market.

C.G. BEANS
1915 Central Avenue, Evanston 60201. Telephone 475-4455. Hours: M–F 9:30–6:30, SAT 9–5. Customers can be placed on a free mailing list by signing up at the store or sending in a request.

C. G. Beans features thirty-five different coffee blends and beans, including eleven Swiss water-processed decaffeinated coffees. Their selection of teas is even larger, fifty-six in all, including several that, like the coffees, have had the caffeine removed. Still rather small and new, C. G. Beans has put together a product lineup of coffee-brewing and bean-grinding equipment from such makers as Melitta, Braun, Simac and Chemex. Imported spices, cookies and candies are a newer sideline. As for their coffees, fresh shipments come in weekly and are stored in airtight containers to preserve freshness and retard oxidation.

COFFEE CHICAGO LTD.
801 North Wabash Avenue, Chicago 60610. Telephone 664-6415. Hours: M–F 7:30–6.

A combination shop and cafe, Coffee Chicago is located not far from a subway stop and Michigan Avenue, so professionals on the way to or from work can stop in to pick up a coffee to go or a bag of beans or tea or a slice of cake. About fifteen to sixteen varieties of coffee and twenty-four teas are offered. Prices run medium to high.

THE COFFEE CORNER
Laundry Mall Shopping Plaza, 566 Chestnut Street, Winnetka 60093. Telephone: 441-0530. Hours: M–F 10–5:30, SAT 9:30–5.

Tucked into the Laundry Mall Shopping Plaza, Coffee Corner is fine for a broad selection of special blends. Featured are three house blends; one which combines four different beans has become the most popular. The AM blend is a dark roast, while the PM blend is described as a Scandinavian type. In addition to fresh beans and teas, Coffee Corner rounds out its inventory with coffee brewers and supplies, an assortment of kitchen gadgets, towels and imported biscuits. It's a handsome store with hardwood floors and brick walls adding to the natural, countrylike atmosphere.

THE COFFEE DROP SHOP
12 North Third Street, St. Charles 60174. Telephone 584-7989. Hours: M–SAT 10–5, SUN noon–5.

The Coffee Drop Shop offers a variety of specialty-grind coffees for tasting demonstrations, in addition to its retail sales of coffees and teas. The store owners are also the only ones in the Fox Valley area to roast their own beans. They will sell beans whole or ground to order. In addition, the store stocks more than twenty different varieties of teas—loose, bagged and instant. They also will serve any of their flavors hot to customers during the winter months, or iced in summer weather. The Coffee Drop Shop also sells major brands of gourmet coffee makers, grinders, etc. They feature a variety of Viennese-style pastries and even bagels. Their entire line of coffees and teas is also available by mail order.

THE COFFEE GOURMET
386 Montclair, Glen Ellyn 60137. Telephone 790-0222. Hours: M–F 8:30–4:30. Monthly mailer is available free by request.

The people at The Coffee Gourmet say that what distinguishes it from other specialty coffee shops is the care they take to insure freshness. It starts with ordering; they buy their coffees in smaller lots, never more than in fifteen-pound orders. After roasting, the beans are kept in air-tight freezer bags (which is how you should store your coffee at home). So you will never find beans out in bins, which may

look quaint, but allows coffee to lose freshness within three to five days. In fact, the beans at The Coffee Gourmet will still be frozen when they leave the store. And they promise delivery within twenty-four hours in Chicago or suburbs, for goods ordered Monday through Thursday. Among special services, the store will keep on file a record of your personal blends. Thus, you can be sure of consistency, once you find that perfect blend for your tastes. In addition to coffee and the accessories needed to grind and brew it, the store stocks a variety of teas, and even has a line of bulk candies. They will prepare custom gift baskets, or you may order from stock designs.

THE COFFEE AND TEA EXCHANGE
3300 North Broadway, Chicago 60657. Telephone 528-2241. Hours: M–F 9–7, SAT 9–6, SUN noon–5.

Since 1978, the Coffee and Tea Exchange has been roasting high-quality coffees on the premises, every day, but never on Sunday. The store has a relaxed atmosphere and knowledgeable staff members who are always willing to talk coffees. Because of the volume of business they do in supplying restaurants and other institutional clients as well as retail customers, most of their coffees are turned over two to three times a week. Coffees from around the world are blended in one or more of the four types offered: Full city/American, Viennese, French and Espresso). The Coffee and Tea Exchange also sells water-processed decaffeinated coffee, fresh roasted and available as a French roast or as a Colombian light roast. Several varieties of flavored coffees are sold, both with and without caffeine, though these are not blended on the premises. As for teas, The Coffee and Tea Exchange has a wide variety of black, semifermented, green and herbal teas, as well as better quality herbs and spices. They also sell grinding and brewing equipment from most major makers as well as imported Italian cappuccino/espresso machines.

COLOR ME COFFEE
3000 North Sheffield Avenue, Chicago 60657. Telephone 935-7669. Hours: M–F 7–6:30, SAT–SUN 10–7.

A new shop and coffee bar near the North Side's Illinois Masonic medical complex looks like a good bet for becoming a source of beans for the professionals in the area. Coffees are roasted on the premises and prices are reasonable. A good supply of coffee- and tea-brewing machines lines the walls. At the coffee bar you can sample the brew of the day and choose from a few pastries and cakes. Outdoor tables invite leisurely sipping in the summer.

THE COOK'S CUPBOARD
1931 West 95th Street, Chicago 60617. Telephone 239-5757. Hours: M–W, F 9–6, TH 9–8, SAT 10–6, SUN 8–1. Small catalog available for mail ordering.

Coffee, tea, herbs and spices line the walls of this relatively new shop in the south suburbs. Over twenty kinds of coffees are offered as well as coffee-making equipment. Teas include gyokuro, a Japanese green tea, and lapsang souchong, a smoky Chinese black tea. A few preserves, spices and chocolate items round out the selection.

THE JAVA EXPRESS
10701 South Hale Avenue, Chicago 60643. Telephone 233-8557 or 239-0912. Hours: M 7–12, TU–F 6–6, SAT 7–6.

Located in a ninety-year-old former pharmacy across from a South Side commuter train station, this combination shop and cafe does a brisk business early in the morning. Freshly roasted and ground coffees are sold in bulk as well as teas and baked goods such as bagels, croissants and cheesecakes. Some imported gourmet food items line the walls. Sidewalk tables in the summer make sipping coffee a pleasure in this attractive Beverly area on the South Side.

Cooking Classes

The cooking boom of the 1970s and early 1980s created an explosion of excellent cooking classes. But since then, the number of people enrolling in cooking classes has steadily declined, forcing some cooking schools to close their doors and others to cut back on the number of classes offered. According to some food experts, the decline is due not so much to a lack of interest in cooking, but because those who enrolled in cooking classes in the 70s have switched their interests to fitness and aerobics classes in the 80s.

Whether that is true or not, the interest in fitness is certainly reflected in the kinds of cooking classes offered in cookware shops, department stores and adult education programs. Seafood, for example, is very popular. French cooking has been replaced by an interest in Oriental cooking, including Japanese, Chinese and even Thai, while vegetarian classes are holding their own.

The list of cooking classes that follows is not all-inclusive. We have merely tried to give a well-balanced sample of the classes available, including those for professional cooks.

Some of the stores listed in the Cookware chapter, such as Cuisine Unlimited, also sponsor cooking classes. And for Chinese instruction, check out the Oriental Food Market and Cooking School in the Ethnic Foods section.

THE CALICO COOK
Monnacep-Oakton Community College, PO Box 367, Skokie 60077. Telephone 982-9888.

Diane Leo is The Calico Cook and she has more than fourteen years experience as a cooking instructor, writer and speaker. Most of her teaching is done through the adult education program of Oakton Community College with courses in cooking for singles, cooking for company, and food processor cookery. Classes are held at various locations depending on the course being taught. Classes may be either demonstration or participation and are limited to twenty-five students maximum. Seasonal courses are taught on a regular basis.

CARSON PIRIE SCOTT & CO.
1 South State Street, Chicago 60602. Telephone 744-2294.

Noon hour classes and demonstrations by well-known guests, cookbook authors and local teachers as well as evening classes in the Level 6 Kitchentech. Schedule available.

CLEA'S CASTLE
1201 Fairoaks Avenue, Oak Park 60302. Telephone 383-8245.

Cleatis Wilcox teaches a wide spectrum of courses for the home cook as well as the budding professional. Classes include cake decorating, baking, pulled-sugar and other candy-making techniques as well as buffet catering, Chinese cuisine, seafoods and even winemaking. A testimonial to her success is the fact that in a recent eighteen-month period, her students won twenty-four medals from a competition sponsored by the American Culinary Federation. Wilcox's own experience includes work as a professional chef and pastry maker. Classes, demonstration and participation are limited to six students. Seasonal courses are held in the baking of holiday treats and specialties. Fees vary.

COOKING AND HOSPITALITY INSTITUTE OF CHICAGO
858 North Orleans Street, Chicago 60610. Telephone 944-0882.

A variety of classes ranging from stocks and sauces, vegetables, boning, filleting, desserts for nonprofessionals. Fees range from $20 to $40. Also classes for professionals leading to two-year degree with fees from $1000 to $3300.

COOK'S WORLD
Randhurst Shopping Center, 999 Elmhurst Road, Mt. Prospect 60056. Telephone 577-0680.

Occasional guest instructors and local teachers offer day and evening classes on topics from Jewish cooking to food processor cooking. Fees range from $10 to $20. Schedule available.

COOKING CRAFT
300 West Main, St. Charles 60174. Telephone 377-1730.
Cooking Craft is a cooking school with a retail shop attached. Subjects taught vary from food processor expertise to the creation of specialty menus. Classes might include vegetarian, Mexican or Oriental at any given time. For holidays, instructors led by owner Jean Becker teach special techniques such as the construction of a panoramic Easter egg, a gingerbread house or making elaborate holiday candies. The school is also widely known for its chocolate show, a demonstration of molding, dipping and tasting. The shop provides free demonstrations on a regular basis, with special programs for larger groups by appointment. Twenty students maximum for class. Demonstration and participation are available; class fees usually are around $6 per session, although many programs are free.

DEBORAH JEAN VEGETARIAN COOKING SCHOOL
33 East Cedar, Chicago 60611. Telephone 280-8042.
Deborah Sisman specializes in meatless cookery, and only uses naturally processed ingredients. She also shuns food colorings and preservatives and urges her students to do everything from scratch. Her courses stress nutrition and weight control, with a goal of helping students understand the effects foods have on health and body development. Classes are participatory and limited to five to ten students. $20 per session.

ELAINE GONZALES COOKING CLASSES
Telephone 498-3971. Rates and class information on request.
When it comes to learning to cook Mexican, Spanish or the like, most experts in and around Chicago immediately think of Elaine Gonzales. All of her classes, usually held in specialty cookware shops such as Cook's World, are for small groups of no more than fifteen if the session is participation or twenty or more students if the class is demonstration. Elaine's classes are usually keyed to the season, with special emphasis on chocolate techniques and artistry, food decorating, as well as the instruction in Spanish or Mexican preparations. Elaine will create classes for laymen or professionals, depending upon the need at a given time or place.

ESS GEZUNDT
555 West Cornelia, Chicago 60657. Telephone 472-3475.

"Eat in good health," says Peggy Marc, owner-instructor of Ess Gezundt. Her specialty is traditional Jewish foods of Eastern Europe, such as gefilte fish made from scratch, challah baking, kreplach and cholent, the simmered Jewish version of cassoulet. While her recipes are based on traditional sources, her techniques include the use of modern kitchen equipment ranging from food processors to microwave ovens. Class size is limited to six to ten students for both participation and demonstration. A typical course consists of six weekly lessons, each lasting for about three hours. Fees vary.

FRANCIS W. PARKER EVENING CLASSES
330 West Webster Avenue, Chicago 60614. Telephone 549-5904.

Adult education classes are offered evenings at this North Side private school, including ethnic, chocolate cookery, wine appreciation and many more. Some classes are taught in the area's home kitchens. Fees range for one-time demonstrations to six-week series from $15 to $35 plus lab fees. Schedule available.

THE FRENCH KITCHEN
3427 West 63rd Street, Chicago 60629. Telephone 776-6715 or 737-3529.

Owner-instructor Lorraine Hooker offers courses in French haute cuisine and cuisine bourgeoise. Although she has been a student at such prestigious schools as La Varenne, Hooker takes the approach that serious cookery can also be fun. As she describes a typical class: "We sip a little wine and exchange and share!" Seasonal courses include le fête du printemps, in which work with lamb and other springtime foods is emphasized. Courses are taught in the kitchen of the restaurant which bears the name of the cooking school. Demonstration classes for up to thirty students cost $10 per lesson. Classes are held on Monday evenings only.

JACALYN LINKO'S COOKING SCHOOL
1610 Dobson, Evanston 60202. Telephone 869-7894.

Linko is a former social worker who became fascinated by cooking and eventually studied in France with Madeleine Kamman, although her repertoire also includes the cuisines of other countries, such as Mexico and Italy. In her ethnic classes she discusses geography, culture and history as they relate to a country's foods and dietary habits. Classes include lecture and demonstration (limited to eight students) and participation (maximum four students). Costs range from $15 for a single demonstration session to $60 for full participation in a course. Seasonal specials include an Eastern European holiday baking course.

THE KITCHEN OF PENELOPE
3500 North Cicero Avenue, Chicago 60641. Telephone 725-7455.

The Penelope of Homeric times may have woven her tapestries while Odysseus was away, but today's Penelope Holden spends her time cooking and teaching cooking. Her specialty is Grecian cuisine, sauces, phyllo pastries, breads, entrees and the like. Classes are usually limited to October and May. The rest of the time Penelope is busy with a Greek catering business. Ten students maximum for each participation class. Classes are always held in a commercial kitchen; students take home samples of their work after each lesson.

LA NUOVA CUCINA ITALIANA
647 Sheridan Square, Evanston 60202. Telephone 328-4443.

No one can meet cooking instructor Maria Battaglia without feeling happy. Her bright personality is reflected in her style of teaching the foods of Italy, emphasizing quick and simple fare from all regions of the country. She makes frequent trips to Italy, studying with teachers such as Marcella Hazan and bringing back regional recipes to share with her students. Battaglia also does extensive professional product consulting. Full participation courses cost $30 per student, per class, for a series of three classes. In addition, Maria occasionally leads summer study tours to Italy.

LA VENTURE COOKING SCHOOL
PO Box 1805, Skokie 60077. Telephone 679-8845.

Owner-instructor Sandra Bisceglie believes food must look good if it is to taste good. Thus, she stresses the importance of appearance in the recipes and techniques she teaches. Her courses are geared primarily for people who want to learn candy making and pastry baking. In addition to teaching classic European recipes, she also conducts a course in Chinese baking. Participation courses are limited to eight to ten students. Course costs begin at $20. Seasonal classes are taught for major holiday festival cooking.

LIVE & LEARN PROGRAM OF THE LATIN SCHOOL
Locations vary. Telephone 664-8760.
Evening and weekend classes on a wide variety of topics including children's classes, holiday cooking and classes from area chefs. Fees from $15. Call for a schedule.

THE PERSIMMON TREE
127 South Third Street, Geneva 60134. Telephone 232-6446.
This is one of the most popular general cooking schools in the western suburbs. Only single-session classes are given, but they are frequent, well organized and vast in range. Local instructors, and from time to time those with national or international reputations, are brought in to lecture and demonstrate technique and method. Courses range from pizza making to wine tastings. The Persimmon Tree also stocks and sells kitchen equipment, specialty coffees, teas and chocolates among other items. Classes cost $16 a session; most are demonstration, although a few participatory sessions are held depending upon interest and subject matter. Class size limited to twenty-three maximum. Detailed course listing catalogs are mailed out on request.

ORIENTAL FOOD MARKET AND COOKING SCHOOL
2801 West Howard, Chicago 60645. Telephone 274-2826.
This is the Chicago area's best-known Oriental cooking school, and its largest. Although owners Chu-Yen Luke and Pansy Luke grew up in the tradition of Chinese cooking, they also teach Japanese, Thai, Korean and other cuisines of the Orient. The school is adjacent to the Lukes' Oriental grocery store, which makes shopping that much easier for any unusual ingredients you may need to practice your lessons. Most classes are demonstration, with limited participation. Classes can be as large as seventy-five students. Rates are $75 for a six week, once a week course or $18 per lesson on a Saturday special course.

PAMELA SIDOCK
2220 North Clark Street, Chicago 60014. Telephone 348-8560.
With a background that includes hands-on study in Italy, Sidock conducts small, personalized courses specializing in the foods of northern Italy. Each session concludes with a four-course dinner that her students have prepared under her supervision. She stresses the use of fresh, high-quality ingredients and gives plenty of personal attention to each student. Both demonstration and participation classes are conducted, each limited to no more than seven students. Specialty courses include a festival dinner offering traditional Italian holiday dishes.

RUTH LAW'S WHAT'S COOKING
PO Box 323, Hinsdale 60521. Telephone 986-1595.

Ruth Law has traveled extensively in the Orient, particularly in China, and is a graduate of Taipei's Wei Chun Cooking School. Her primary concern is to teach the basics of Chinese and Oriental techniques with emphasis on such skills as handling a cleaver, stir-frying and basket-steaming. With that background, says Law, students have the confidence to open any Chinese cookbook and try even the most exotic recipes. Specialized classes include basic wok technique, dim sum and regional cuisines such as Szechwan and Hunan. Seasonal courses cover Chinese holiday buffets, great brunching Chinese-style, Chinese barbecue and so forth. Demonstration classes are limited to twelve to fifteen students, participation classes to eight.

WILLIAMS-SONOMA
17 East Chestnut Street, Chicago 60610. Telephone 642-1592.
Oakbrook Center, Oak Brook 60521. Telephone 789-2702.

This San Francisco-based cookware chain recently began a demonstration cooking school in the Chicago area, featuring nationally known guest teachers and local teachers on a variety of subjects. Schedule available.

WILTON ENTERPRISES
2240 West 75th Street, Woodridge 60517. Telephone 963-7100.

The same company that produces cake decorating books also offers year-round classes for beginners and advanced students in the Wilton method of decorating and the Continental method. Fee is $125 to $500 for one- and two-week courses. Candy classes are also available.

Wine Classes

Other occasional wine classes are taught at The Cooking and Hospitality Institute of Chicago, Francis Parker School, Latin School's Live & Learn program, Northwestern University and Esser's wine shop.

CHICAGO WINE SCHOOL
1633 North Halsted Street, Chicago 60614. Telephone 266-9463.

   Chicago Magazine wine columnist Patrick Fegan teaches beginning, advanced and professional wine classes and seminars. Each class often includes ten or more types of wines for discussion and tasting, covering all wine-growing regions of the world. Fees range from $15 for seminars to $120 to $300 for series.

Professional Cooking Schools

The following schools offer one- to two-year certificates or associate degrees in professional cooking.

CITY COLLEGES OF CHICAGO
30 East Lake Street, Chicago 60601. Telephone 781-9430.

COOKING AND HOSPITALITY INSTITUTE
858 North Orleans Street, Chicago 60610. Telephone 944-0882.

DUMAS PERE
1129 Depot Street, Glenview 60625. Telephone 729-4823.

HARPER COLLEGE
Algonquin and Roselle roads, Palatine 60067. Telephone 397-3000 ext. 522.

JOLIET JUNIOR COLLEGE
1216 Houbolt Avenue, Joliet 60436. Telephone 815-729-9020, ext. 255.

KENDALL COLLEGE
2408 Orrington Avenue, Evanston 60202. Telephone 886-1300.

LEXINGTON INSTITUTE
10840 South Western Avenue, Chicago 60643. Telephone 779-3800. For women.

TRITON COLLEGE
2000 5th Avenue, River Grove 60171. Telephone 456-0300, ext. 387.

WASHBURNE TRADE SCHOOL
3233 West 31st Street, Chicago 60623. Telephone 650-4400.

Municipal Classes

A variety of adult and children's cooking classes also are offered by the following cities and schools:

CITY OF EVANSTON RECREATION DEPARTMENT
Telephone 855-2910. Locations vary.

COLLEGE OF DU PAGE
425 22nd Street, Glen Ellyn 60237. Telephone 858-2800, ext. 2208.

ELK GROVE PARK DISTRICT
620 Rusking Drive, Elk Grove Village 60007. Telephone 437-8780.

MONNACEP PROGRAM OF OAKTON COMMUNITY COLLEGE
Locations vary in Maine Township and Niles. Telephone 982-9888.

NEW TRIER EXTENSION
Locations vary in Winnetka and Northfield. Telephone 256-7070.

WINNETKA COMMUNITY HOUSE
620 Lincoln Avenue, Winnetka 60093. Telephone 446-0537.

Cookware

The French call their assembly of kitchen equipment a *batterie de cuisine*, which sounds somewhat like military hardware. Even though the cook, not the cookware, creates the finished product, certain basic equipment is essential to produce the variety of dishes that most of today's serious cooks wish to prepare. You can improvise for steaming without buying a woven Chinese steaming basket, although they are nice to have and a handsome way to present kuo teh. A *bain marie* can be made using two different sized sauce or baking pans; similarly a double boiler easily can be jerry-rigged.

But, there's no way to get around the need for sharply honed knives and other cutlery that holds an edge. Heavy bottom saucepans and skillets not only last forever, but distribute heat more uniformly than do cheaper inferiors found in variety and discount stores. Most of the vast array of equipment and utensils many cooks seek these days, however, is only found in cookware shops and similar specialty stores. M. F. K. Fisher may have written about a wonderful cook who used nothing more complicated than a fork, but for most of us, a bit more is called for in the way of a batterie de cuisine.

Also look for name-brand cookware at the State Street stores of Carson Pirie Scott and Marshall Field. See the Ethnic Foods chapter for more ethnic cookware.

CORRADO CUTLERY

26 North Clark Street, Chicago 60602. Telephone 368-8450. Hours: M–F 9–5, SAT 10–4:30.

The story of Corrado Cutlery is almost a family saga. The business was started in 1905 when Chicago barber Carmen Corrado decided to open a small knife sharpening and grinding shop, which also sold knives and razors. That small beginning gave birth to the flourishing business that has been carried on by the Corrado sons. Their store is still located in the heart of Chicago's Loop and the old walnut fixtures, though marked by the passage of time and use, establish the continuity upon which Corrado Cutlery has built its reputation. This may be the most complete cutlery shop in the Midwest. A linchpin of their stock is the complete lines of such houses as Henckels professionaal and home knives and cutlery. Other imported makes include Wusthof-Trident and Dreizack Solingen. Their vast inventory includes a full selection of poultry shears, kitchen shears, sharpening hones (including diamond hones) and other selected cooking accessories. A hallmark of their old-fashioned service is extensive advice and consultation. This is a unique store in American merchandising today, recognized by professionals in the food field for the quality of its stock and the experience of its sales people.

THE CHEF'S CATALOG

3925 Commercial Avenue, Northbrook 60062. Telephone 480-9400. Retail hours: M–SAT 10:30–4. Catalog is available by mail; $2 for annual subscription of five issues.
New retail outlet also at Crossroads Shopping Center, Highland Park 60035. Telephone: 831-1100. Hours: M–F 10–9, SAT 10–6, SUN 11–5.

Orders from The Chef's Catalog have actually been shipped to the North Pole! No, we don't think the customer was "you know who." But when the White House needs specialty cookware, they'll contact The Chef's Catalog. So do Bo Derek and Danny Kaye. The Chef's Catalog lists over a thousand kitchenwares, fine foodstuffs and imaginative gifts from around the world. They boast that they sell professional restaurant equipment for the home chef and just a glance through a current edition shows how true that is. You'll find items ranging from basting

brushes to an electric mincer. Foodstuffs include wares from New York's Silver Palate and name-brand equipment from such top-of-the-line makers as Krups, Calphalon and Mouli. The Chef's Catalog does not discount, but quality is guaranteed and the selection of wares is enormous. In addition to their mail-order catalog, they also have a warehouse walk-in store for across-the-counter trade.

COOK'S WORLD
Randhurst Shopping Center, 999 Elmhurst Road, Mt. Prospect 60056. Telephone 577-0680. Hours: M–F 10–9, SAT 10–5:30, SUN 11–5. Free placement on mailing list.

Supplies, gadgets and classes are just a few of the attractions at Cook's World. The inventory runs the gamut from food processors and accessories to restaurant-quality cookware, slicers, grinders, coffee makers, cutlery, glassware, scales, mitts, pots and woks. Among food supplies, shoppers will find imported and domestic cooking chocolates, vinegars, mustards, spices, and so forth. For the student cook, regular classes bring in experts in various culinary disciplines to demonstrate and discuss methods and techniques.

CUISINE UNLIMITED
7871 Taft Street, Merrillville, Indiana 46410. Telephone (219) 738-2443. Hours: M–SAT 10–5:30, class nights until 9:30, extended hours for the month before Christmas. Call, write, or drop into the store to get on the free mailing list for class information and a store catalog.

Cuisine Unlimited offers what the serious cook needs: support, supplies and instruction. You won't find giftwares here, unless you are giving something to someone who truly appreciates what it takes to cook well. Nothing is stocked before a prototype is tested in the store's kitchen, showing a dedication to principle not often seen in modern retailing. Thus, if customers want to see how something works, be it gadget or a major piece of equipment, they are given a go-around in the test kitchen. This thoroughness extends not only to the usual stainless-steel pots, enamelware and gadgets, but to the more esoteric ethnic cookware, such as pizzelle irons, pasta makers and the like. Cuisine Unlimited may also be only one of a few, if not the only outlet for a little gadget called the Form-a-Tart. It does what the name implies, removing some of the difficulty even experienced bakers can have in making perfectly round, mini tart shells. When it comes to foodstuffs, the store stocks freshly roasted coffee beans, teas and spices plus an ecletic array of items like chutneys, semolina flour, fruited vinegars and Oriental seasonings. And, yes, Cuisine Unlimited hosts some of the area's better-known cooking instructors for a diversity of classes, from those for the budding professional to a Kids Kooking Korner for students who can hardly see over the countertop without a step stool.

CRATE AND BARREL

Warehouse Store: 1510 North Wells, Chicago 60610. Telephone 787-5900.
850 North Michigan Avenue, Chicago 60611. Telephone 372-0100.
1515 Sheridan Road, Wilmette 60091. Telephone 256-2723.
Oak Brook Shopping Center, Oakbrook 60521. Telephone 986-1300.
Hawthorne Shopping Center, Vernon Hills 60061. Telephone 367-1333.
1240 Northbrook Court, Northbrook 60062. Telephone 272-8920.
Woodfield Mall, Schaumburg 60193. Telephone 885-4200.
Old Orchard Mall, Skokie 60077. Telephone 674-6850.
Hours vary at various stores. To be placed on free mailing list, fill out an address card at any store.

Crate and Barrel is one of the most brilliant ideas in American merchandising. Highly polished hardwood floors and wood or high-tech shelving highlight an array of merchandise distinguished by simplicity of design, high quality and reasonable prices. Founded in 1962 in Chicago's then trendy Old Town area, the store caught on with those shoppers looking for good design and practicality. Since then, Crate and Barrel has opened many branches and developed a huge inventory that runs the gamut from Calphalon and Lentrade to French copper, bakeware, gadgets, electrical appliances and serving accessories. The stores are also noted for the depth of their selections of dinnerware and stemware, and other items for the creative shopper, such as Marimekko textiles. The seconds room is terrific for discovering bargains in glassware and the like. In some respects, shopping at Crate and Barrel is like browsing through a museum housing all that is contemporary and well designed for America's kitchens and dining areas.

ESSENTIALS
Ice House, 200 Applebee Street, Barrington 60010. Telephone 381-5303. Hours: M–W, F–SAT 9:30–5:30, TH 9:30–8:30, SUN 11–4. Mailing list registry available at store.

Shoppers will see a great gadget display at Essentials, where the emphasis is on convenience and customer service. This is, after all, a small operation, yet, they stock some big names in the field of cookware: Calphalon, Krups, Cuisinart and Chicago Metallic Bakeware among them. Gourmet specialties include sauces from Postillion, Silver Palate and Foodstuffs (q.v.), imported chocolates and other candies as well as diabetic sweets. Custom gift wraps, a bridal registry and delivery, plus cooking demonstrations each Saturday, are all part of the personal service that makes Essentials a favorite for kitchen needs.

FREELING POT AND PAN
5210 South Harper Court, Chicago 60615. Telephone 643-8080. Hours: M–SAT 10–6.

Downstairs one finds linens and glassware, and upstairs (you have to go outside and up the stairs to get there) is a nice selection of cookware, baking supplies and bins of coffee and tea in this shop in the middle of Hyde Park. Such top-of-the-line brands as Calphalon and Paderno mix with plain old cast iron in the pan selections. There is also a good supply of the latest cooking gadgets, and some cookbooks.

THE GREAT ACE
2818 North Broadway Avenue, Chicago 60657. Telephone 348-0705. Hours: M–F 9:30–9, SAT 9–7, SUN 10–6.

This is a hardware store, but not like most. Skip the main floor and head for the second, where you'll find tableware, glassware, china, linens, bakeware, a full line of electric gadgets, including food processors, as well as pots and pans. The lineup is irresistible. Watch for sales, when normal retail prices are often slashed dramatically.

HOFFRITZ FOR CUTLERY
634 North Michigan Avenue, Chicago 60611. Telephone 664-4473. Hours: M–SAT 10–6, SUN noon–5.
835 North Michigan Avenue, Chicago 60610. Telephone 787-6839. Houurs: M–W 10–6, TH 10–7, F–SAT 10–6, SUN noon–5.

A manufacturer of a line of excellent kitchen knives, this chain of small shops also offers other brands than Hoffritz, including Henckels, Chicago Cutlery and Sabatier. The Hoffritz knives are often on sale, sometimes as much as 50 percent off, so it may pay to wait. Some other kitchen gadgets, including wine openers, scissors and gift items are sold here, too.

THE HOUSE ON THE HILL

PO Box 221, River Forest. 60305. Telephone 344-3136. All orders are filled by mail only. Write or call for a free catalog which describes and illustrates the designs available.

A labor of love aptly describes what Caroline Kallas is doing. She has devoted herself to the manufacture and reproduction of antique German springerle cookie molds. These are made by an almost obsolete printing plate process which results in a one-quarter-inch metal face mounted on a three-quarter-inch thick cherrywood backing. Each mold is painstakingly copied from the original, so that if the original had a slight scratch in the design, so too will the copy. Time was when nineteenth-century cooks would use the molds to make cookies for Christmas tree ornaments. Now, many people just buy the molds as decorations for a country kitchen look, but they are as usable as the originals were more than a century ago.

K. A. VOGEL & SONS

2215 North Milwaukee Avenue, Chicago 60647. Telephone 235-5336. Hours: M–F 8–4:30, SAT 8–12.

This seventy-five-year-old firm manufactures, sells and sharpens cutlery. Prices on Henckels, Case, Clauss and Marks brands are reasonable.

KITCHEN BOUTIQUE

407 Coffin Road, Long Grove 60047. Telephone 634-9019. Hours: M–F 10–4, SAT 10–3, SUN 12–5.

The owner of this bustling shop claims she started her business thirteen years ago to get out of the house. "Look at me now!," she says, undoubtedly with deserved entrepreneurial pride. The store is stuffed with all kinds of kitchen gadgets not to mention more serious culinary needs. Shoppers will find assortments of pots and pans, carbon steel cutlery, copperware, peppermills and salt cellars, bar accessories, aprons, hot mitts, kitchen towels, canister and spice storage sets, cookbooks, recipe cards and storage boxes.

THE MERRY COOKER

2829 North Clybourn Avenue, Chicago 60618. Telephone 477-5504. Hours: M–SAT 8–5.

The Merry Cooker is a division of a seventy-five-year-old restaurant supply house, Krasny & Company. So, while the retail store only has been in business since 1982, it is able to draw upon the vast resources and professional suppliers of its parent company. The Merry Cooker is a good source for Lodge cast-iron cookware and unusual kitchen gadgets. If you have been unable to find a particular kitchen tool, this might be the place to check. They have a large mail-order business and you can order from their catalog which is revised regularly. To get on the mailing list, telephone or write for a free listing.

NORTHWESTERN CUTLERY SUPPLY

810 West Lake Street, Chicago 60607. Telephone 421-3666. Hours: M–F 7–4, SAT 7–2:30.

For over fifty years, this firm has sold brand-name cutlery at discounted prices. Henckels, Gerber, Chicago Cutlery and Forstner are just some of the brands of kitchen knives you can find here. The company is located near the Randolph Street Market.

OTTO POMPER

109 South Wabash Avenue, Chicago 60603. Telephone 372-0881. Hours: M–SAT 10–5.

A tradition in the Loop since 1890, this firm sells top-of-the-line cutlery, including kitchen knives by Henckels, Wusthof-Trident, Gerber and Chicago Cutlery. A small selection of kitchen gadgets, scales, Braun coffee makers and electric gadgets are also part of the selection. Helpful service.

WILLIAMS-SONOMA

17 East Chestnut Street, Chicago 60610. Telephone 642-1593. Hours: M–W 10–6, TH 10–7, F 10–6, SAT 10–5:30, SUN noon–4.
Oak Brook Center, Oakbrook 60521. Telephone 789-2702.
Hours: M–F 10–9, SAT 10–5:30, SUN noon–5.

This San Francisco-based cookware shop with a high-quality line of goods for the kitchen is relatively new in the Chicago market. Although the stores are not large, the inventory is usually high quality and sometimes unique. You'll find expensive ice cream machines next to inexpensive French ice cream dishes, top-of-the-line Calphalon pots near simple, blue-and-white-striped kitchen towels. A limited supply of cookbooks is offered. A good place to shop for gifts for cooks.

WOKS 'N' THINGS
2234 South Wentworth Avenue, Chicago 60616. Telephone 842-0701. Hours: SUN–F 9–8, SAT 9–9.

While browsing through Chinatown, a stop here will tempt you to pick up another wok because of the reasonable prices and a range of good choices, from flat-bottomed woks to stainless-steel woks. A good selection of other Oriental utensils such as cleavers, electric rice cookers, bamboo steamers, cookbooks and Mongolian hot pots are available.

Wholesale Cookware

CENTRAL SUPPLY COMPANY
811–813 West Randolph Street, Chicago 60607. Telephone 733-4222. Hours: M–F 9–5, SAT 9–2.

Looking for a giant stockpot or a professional quality baking pan? Head for this Randolph Street Market shop that sells to restaurants and institutions. Don't expect to browse, though, through the jumble of equipment; owner Nick J. Kasimos says he's a busy man and has no time if you don't know exactly what you want. He also carries chinaware, glassware and silverware.

CHEF'S EDGE
1139 West Madison Avenue, Chicago 60607. Telephone 733-2530. Hours: M–F 8:30–5:30, SAT 9–3.

In this restaurant-supply store west of the Loop, you'll find the basics from stockpots to knives at competitive prices.

KRASNY SUPPLY COMPANY
538 North Milwaukee Avenue, Chicago 60622. Telephone 733-4920. Hours: M–F 8–4:30.

Here's a wholesale business west of the Loop that's turned more of its attention to retail customers. The attractive display area is more than most wholesale supply companies offer the home cook, not to mention friendly service. Owners say prices are often 30 percent less than regular retail cookware shops. Stockpots, Calphalon pots and pans, glassware, chinaware and sturdy commercial kitchen gadgets can be found here, as well as some electrical appliances. The staff is willing to answer questions.

Dairy Products

Chicago is just south of Wisconsin, the dairy state, and we take good advantage of our proximity to such bounty. Golden yellow cheddar cheese, colby longhorn, not to mention domestic versions of feta, mozzarella and other European varieties are well stocked in both supermarkets and specialty shops.

Other products readily available include imported cheeses, butterfat rich ice creams, yogurts and crème fraîche, not to mention ninety-three score butter, heavy creams and Grade A milk.

Cheese

We'll bet you cannot walk into a cheese shop or past a cheese counter without stopping for a nibble of something, even though you know exactly what you intend to buy. Tasting is part of the fun of buying fresh cheeses, cut from the round or the block by a clerk who really knows the difference between a parmesan and an asiago or a camembert and a brie. You can easily find people who are as strongly partisan about specific cheeses as oenophiles are about their favorite wines.

Many cheeses are produced in large factories but are quite good nonetheless. Others are almost handmade, whether made in small wheels or found hanging in netting from a ceiling hook.

Virtually all cheese we eat is made from cow's, sheep's or goat's milk. (The taste for goat's cheese, such as French chèvre, is especially growing by leaps and bounds.) The milk is separated into solids and liquids (Little Miss Muffet's curds and whey). The solid curds can be left to ferment and age on their own, although more often than not a friendly bacteria is introduced to hasten the process. But a good deal of labor is involved in making most cheeses; while Father Time gets some of the credit, he gets some human help, too.

While there are literally hundreds of cheeses, there are only four basic kinds:

soft, semi-soft, firm and hard, ranging from a cream cheese easily spread with the flat blade of a knife, to a hard pecorino or parmesan. Each cheese has its own unique attributes, and with some study and attention you should easily know your cheeses from abertam to zsendice.

Also for cheese, shop the various department stores such as Marshall Field and Neiman-Marcus and specialty shops (listed in Gourmet & Takeout Foods chapter) such as Zambrana's, Foodstuffs in Glencoe and Treasure Island supermarkets. One of the city's best selections of chèvre can be found at Mitchell Cobey Cuisine, along with a full line of French cheeses. For Italian cheeses see listings in the Ethnic Foods chapter for Convito Italiano, Rex Imported Italian Foods and Riviera Market.

CHALET WINE & CHEESE SHOPS
405 West Armitage Avenue, Chicago 60614. Telephone 266-7155.
3000 North Clark Street, Chicago 60657. Telephone 935-9400.
40 East Delaware Street, Chicago 60610. Telephone 787-8555.
444 West Fullerton Avenue, Chicago 60614. Telephone 871-0300.
1525 East 53rd Street, Chicago 60615. Telephone 324-5000.
71 Linden, Glencoe 60022. Telephone 835-3900.
Hours vary from shop to shop.

Strong on French cheeses, this chain of stores has a policy of letting customers taste any cheese before purchase. And because of the large selection, about three hundred varieties, tasting is truly a good idea. Chalet has a larger range than most department stores in Chicago of soft-ripened French cheeses. Danish, German, Italian and American cheeses, including a fine herkimer from New York State, are also carried. Sheep and goats' milk cheeses are available, too. A full line of domestic and imported crackers, French breads or rolls and sourdough bread from Boudin bakery are fine bases for the cheese. While you're there, don't forget to pick a wine to go with the cheese.

THE CORNER CHEESE SHOP
118 North Third Street, St. Charles 60174. Telephone 584-0990. Hours: 10–5 daily.

This specialty shop routinely stocks over fifty types of cheese, both domestic and imported, plus an assortment of sausage, maple syrups, honey, crackers and other cheese-related items such as serving boards and cutters. In addition, owner Lynne Gibbs schedules regular demonstrations and tastings for up to fifty people in her shop, all at no charge. Inventory will include seasonal items like cheddar cheese shaped into hearts for Valentine's Day. The Corner Cheese Shop also stocks salt-free or low-sodium cheeses for diet-conscious shoppers.

FALBO'S
1335 West Taylor Street, Chicago 60607. Telephone 421-8915. Hours: TU–SAT 9–5:30, SUN 9–2.

As soon as you enter, you'll know this is a cheese shop. The smell doesn't waft; it practically vibrates through your nostrils. Here is well-aged Italian cheese: parmesan, romano, mozzarella, scamorze and more. Those cheeses that are not hanging behind the counter are in the back, in a large storage area for aging and curing. In the old days, the Falbo family actually made their famous cheeses here. But the plant was moved sometime after World War II to a suburb and now the family no longer makes cheeses, not even in the factory. But they certainly know how to sell them. The small store also stocks an array of Italian sausages, pepperonis and similar cured meats, along with some delicious homemade pastas, including ravioli-like small pillows. And there is a selection of imported Italian canned goods, peppers and the like. Even if you don't want to buy, it's great fun just to visit the old Taylor Street neighborhood around Falbo's and taste a little of this and that. At the least, you'll find some good conversation and learn a little about good Italian-style cheeses in the process.

Crème Fraîche

Crème fraîche is a fermentation of cream used as a tangy alternative to whipped cream in French desserts and sauces. Although not easily found in Chicago, a few commercially made brands are available. In addition to Marshall Field and Company (see following listing), also check with Foodworks, Zambrana's and Mitchell Cobey in Chicago, and Foodstuffs in Glencoe. (See chapter on Gourmet & Takeout Foods.)

MARSHALL FIELD & CO.
(Seventh floor gourmet food department.) 111 North State Street, Chicago 60602. Telephone 781-3669. Hours: TU, W, F, SAT 9:45–5:45; M, TH 9:45–7.

Field's stocks a fine California-made crème fraîche from the Kendall Cheese Company, which also makes a variety of goat cheeses. The store also sells a premium house-brand ice cream made by Roney Dairy.

Ice Cream

Chicago is rich with ice cream shops, ranging from the ultra-modern Italian gelateria to the old-fashioned store with stools and marble countertops.

The quality of ice cream is measured by its butterfat content. Most commercial ice creams sold at supermarkets have a low butterfat content, often around 10 percent. Generally, the higher the price, the higher the butterfat and creamy richness. Some of the best custom ice creams will approach 20 percent butterfat, which may not be good for your waistline, but the richness is unforgettable.

Another fact of life about ice creams is that, except for the very best, they are injected with air. This makes them lighter and at the same time bulkier. Dense ice cream is our favorite, with the emphasis less on the ice and more on the cream. The Italian gelatos typify this kind of ice cream that has proven such a favorite.

Natural ice creams are those made without preservatives. The recipe might remind you of the kind you make at home, starting with an egg custard, adding your fruits or other flavors and churning by hand crank or electric motor. Because natural ice creams have no preservatives, they are best eaten within days of purchase, although two or three weeks in the freezer should not significantly diminish their quality.

For other sources of ice cream see Oberweis Dairy in this chapter, Cunis Candies and Universal Candies (Chocolate & Sweets) and Marshall Field (Gourmet & Takeout Foods).

AL GELATO
7434 West North Avenue, Elmwood Park 60635. Telephone 453-9737.
814 Church Street, Evanston 60201. Telephone 869-9133.
Hours: SUN–TH noon–11:30, F–SAT noon–12:30 a.m.
Once you have tasted Al Gelato ice cream, forget about all the awful stuff that often passes for ice cream. More than sixty flavors are made fresh daily using heavy whipping cream, Italian syrups, fresh fruits and nuts, plus imported liqueurs and chocolates. The texture makes the difference. This is a full ice cream, without the injected compressed air that is used by mass-producers. And it is colorful ice cream, perfect for dessert when a certain look is as important as a certain flavor.

DOVE CANDIES & ICE CREAM
6000 South Pulaski, Chicago 60629. Telephone 582-3119.
5172 West 95th, Oak Lawn 60453. Telephone 857-9676.
Hours: 9:30–10:45 daily.
Dove has been a fixture on the South Side since 1939, when Leo Stefanos first opened it. But in recent years, the old-fashioned store with a small candy-making operation in the back has gained notoriety for producing what some call "the best ice cream bar in the world." Leo is gone now, but his wife Sophia and son Michael run the operation. They still hand-dip the bars in high-quality bittersweet chocolate to encase the rich ice creams that come in strawberry, coffee, coconut, chocolate and vanilla flavors. The ice cream, also made in the back of the store, makes a great sundae, especially with Dove's homemade toppings and fresh whipped cream (36 percent butterfat). There's a full line of candies near the cash register, too, to tempt you as you pay the bill.

POMODORO GELATERIA
Northbrook Court, Northbrook 60062. Telephone 480-1077. Hours: M–SAT 11:30–9:30, SUN noon–8.
Adjacent to Pomodoro Restaurant in Northbrook Court, this gelateria is a high-tech mixture of chrome shelves, glass and marble. There is a small area to eat gelato or sip a cup of espresso in the store, but otherwise everything is carry-out. Each day features a dozen flavors of gelato, that dense and creamy ice cream that has become a contemporary favorite. Butterfat content is 14 percent and fruit flavors tend to be the best. Chocolate-chunk versions suffer because of a grade of chocolate that is too dry when showcased against the rich ice cream. The gelato can be purchased in pints or half pints, as well as in hand-rolled waffle cones. Pomodoro Gelateria also stocks pasta so fresh it's still wet, not dried out. Other commodities on the shelves include chunks of asiago cheese, bolognese sauce with meat or sausage, tomato sauce, and a creamy white-wine sauce. In addition, the store offers a wide range of ready-to-go salads, pastries such as homemade cheese-

cakes and flourless chocolate Italian torte, and grinds for espresso and cappuccino. Whatever Pomodoro Gelateria lacks in wide-ranging stock, is offset by its convenient shopping-center location. The shop is fine for a quick trip when you need just a few things, especially ice cream that is beyond the normal chain-store quality.

Milk & Butter

OBERWEIS DAIRY
945 Lake Street, Aurora 60586. Telephone 897-0512. Hours: M–SAT 9–10, SUN 10–1.

Since 1927, Oberweis dairy has been serving customers milk gathered from the surrounding Fox River Valley farms. In many respects, the dairy is like a trip back to that early time. Oberweis still sends out milkmen to deliver products, including glass-bottled milk and a great 36 percent butterfat whipping cream. But in the summer, people like to stop in for the dairy's good ice cream sodas and sundaes and sit at the few tables in front. A glass window separates the ice cream shop from the milk-bottling equipment in the back.

TREASURE ISLAND FOOD STORES
Main office and store, 3460 North Broadway Avenue, Chicago 60657. Telephone 327-4265. Hours: M–F 8–9, SAT 8:30–9, SUN 8:30–6.

Look in any of the eight Treasure Island supermarkets for imported butters from Denmark, the Netherlands and France, all with unique and stronger dairy flavors than American butter. Also, you'll find a commercial, imported Devonshire cream and crème fraîche by Santé. The Dean Dairy whipping cream sold here has not been ultra-pasteurized and thus whips better.

Dried Fruits & Nuts

Remember those hot nut stands in the five-and-dime store? What a treat to buy cashews or Brazil nuts, or if pennies counted, just plain old peanuts. Well, we've come a long way in the dried fruit and nut department!

Now, the idea is to buy by bulk. The stores listed here generally have large bins loaded with those fruits and nuts you'll want for baking or just nibbling. Many will also stock other bulk dry goods, be it candies or flours or grains of one kind or another. Because purchasing is by bulk, you can take only the amount you'll need without worry about waste or spoilage. And, as with so many specialty shops, be sure to ask a salesperson about anything of which you are unsure. Many of these stores have mailing lists. Be sure to get yourself listed so you can learn of unique buying opportunities as they occur.

Ethnic markets, particularly Indian and Middle Eastern, are good sources for buying dried nuts and fruits in bulk. (See Ethnic Foods.) Also check out the listings in the Health Food, Produce, and Spices & Herbs chapters.

NUTS ON CLARK
3830 North Clark Street, Chicago 60613. Telephone 871-8777. Hours: 9–6 daily. They send out regular announcements of seasonal and periodic specials to their mailing list.

If Robert Hall had gone into the nuts, spices and condiments business, instead of clothing, his plain pipe racks would have been replaced by large barrels and other containers. That's the approach at Nuts on Clark, where bulk buying by them means savings of 20 to 30 percent for you. Here's a stock of over nine hundred different kinds of nuts, dried fruits, spices, condiments, candies and chocolates plus coffees, teas, pastas and preserves. A U-shaped counter is totally covered with candy jars and canisters, three and four deep, while hundreds of drums occupy some 2500 feet of floor space. Most of the loose nuts, dried fruits, candies and coffees are sold in half-pound minimums. Nuts can be ordered in most cases raw, roasted, whole or halved. The store stocks as many as sixty different spices and chances are if you can't find it here, you won't find it anywhere. And since foods are kept in bulk containers, it's not too difficult to taste a small sample to make sure you are getting the exact flavoring ingredient you are seeking.

A TASTE OF NATURE
Geneva on the Dam, Geneva 60134. Telephone 232-0030. Hours: M–F 10–5, SAT 9:30–5:30, SUN 11–5.

What began in 1981 as a small enterprise catering at-home parties and selling snack bags for students has mushroomed into an extensive product line of fresh nuts and dried fruits. In addition, A Taste of Nature features homemade popcorn in a variety of flavors; for special orders they will even custom design and paint large popcorn cans. Stock also includes yogurt and carob candies, plus those that are sugar and salt free. They will create custom gift items and centerpieces for dinners and parties.

Ethnic Foods

Chicago is a microcosm of the country as a whole. The city contains practically every ethnic group that has ever settled in the United States; over sixty-five have been identified, according to the city's Department of Human Services. But, while the term melting pot is used to describe how immigrants settled and learned American ways, it's not totally accurate. Luckily for the adventurous cook, ethnic groups tend to stick together in their own neighborhoods and open shops that carry their favorite foods. It's certainly true in Chicago.

Walk down Devon Avenue and, in one stretch, you'll feel like you are in India with shops smelling of saffron and cumin and sari palaces that lend vivid color to the street. Take a trip to Argyle Street and you are in Southeast Asia with small grocery stores filled with lemon grass and fish sauce and fiery hot chili peppers. Drive to 26th Street and you could be in Mexico City with the smell of roasting corn tortillas everywhere.

The following list of shops is by no means complete. The one thing we discovered in exploring the neighborhoods was that this book could not possibly include all ethnic shops. The number of small, hidden grocery stores, bakeries and butchers we found numbered in the hundreds. Many of them had no signs out front or if they did, they weren't in English. Often, no one inside spoke English, either. That's the main problem in shopping ethnic markets, so it's wise to know what you are looking for. Also, be aware that many of the shops may not be as spic and span as the local supermarket. Neither problem should stop you, though, because you'll discover foods you've never seen or tasted before and meet very interesting people along the way.

For other ethnic shops, check the chapters on Baked Goods, Dairy Products, Gourmet & Takeout Food, and Meats. A source for foods from the British Isles is Winston Sausages (see Meats).

Chinese

ORIENTAL FOOD MARKET & COOKING SCHOOL
2801 West Howard Street, Chicago 60645. Telephone 274-2826. Hours: M–F 10–6:30, SAT 9:30–6:30.

If you can't find it at the Oriental Food Market, then there's a good chance you can't find it in any other Chicago Oriental market, either. The owners are knowledgeable and are natural teachers, willingly sharing their expertise with shoppers and students. Lining the shelves are groceries from China, Japan, Thailand, the Philippines and Korea. Some frozen prepared foods and fresh produce also are stocked. A full line of utensils, woks, cleavers, chinaware and Oriental cookbooks complete the stock. One half of the building is a large demonstration kitchen and dining room for cooking classes. The shop is located near Chicago's northern city limits.

NEW QUAN WAH
2217 South Wentworth Street, Chicago 60616. Telephone 225-8285. Hours: W–M 9–6:30.

Arguably the cleanest grocery in Chinatown, this small shop carries a full line of Chinese products, neatly arranged so it's easy to locate what you want. But what draws the Chinese in the neighborhood as well as "outsiders" is the delicious-looking and -smelling array of cooked foods in the small deli in the front. It is hard to resist buying a slab of Chinese barbequed ribs, or roast duck or spicy meatballs, all to go.

PHOENIX COMPANY BAKERY
1133 North Argyle Street, Chicago 60640. Telephone 878–5833. Hours: 10–7 daily.

Tiny combination bakery and takeout in the Thai and Vietnamese neighborhood on Argyle, featuring beautifully roasted ducks and barbecued pork. Typical baked goods include moon cakes and almond cookies.

WAH MAY COMPANY
2410 South Wentworth Avenue, Chicago 60616. Telephone 225-9119. Hours: 9–7 daily.

Entering this shop, located near the south end of Chinatown, is rather like heading into an old-fashioned Oriental bazaar. The sights and sounds and confusion on a busy Saturday are mind boggling. Better go on a calmer weekday, so you can browse at your leisure among the stacks and shelves of sometimes dusty jars and bottles of lychee nuts, black beans, and who knows how many kinds of soy sauce. Fresh produce cases line the back, filled with napa cabbage, Chinese broccoli, bok choy and the like. Equipment and chinaware are stacked haphazardly in another room along with packaged noodles and Chinese desserts.

WAH MAY PLAZA
230 East Cermak Road, Chicago 60616. Telephone 225-9007. Hours: 9–7 daily.

In contrast to the confined and crowded Wah May Company in Chinatown, this sister shop, located just east of Chinatown, is clean, airy and almost modern looking. Carrying basically the same line of Chinese goods as the other store, this one also offers some Vietnamese and Korean foods. Look for a garage entrance; parking within the building makes shopping here a bit easier than in Chinatown.

WAH LEUNG HERB COMPANY
4926 North Broadway Avenue, Chicago 60640. Telephone 271-4922. Hours: 9–7:30 daily.

Around the corner and a block south of Argyle Street, with its mix of Thai and Vietnamese shops, is this supermarketlike Oriental store which carries neat rows of all kinds of Oriental products and a large, fresh-looking array of produce including Thai eggplant, mung beans, several types of mushrooms and dried herbs. The smoked, barbecued ducks hanging near the doorway are too tempting to pass up.

Dutch

THE DUTCH STORE
3245 West 111th Street, Chicago 60617. Telephone 238-3927. Hours: M–SAT 10–5.

Imported, packaged foods such as jellies by Betowe, cane syrup, cookies and other foods are sold in this small, southwest side shop that deals in all imported Dutch items. One can also find fine quality gouda and edam cheeses and friendly service from the owners.

German

KUHN'S DELICATESSEN AND LIQUORS

3053 North Lincoln Avenue, Chicago 60657. Telephone 525-9019 or 525-4595. Hours: M–TH 9:30–7, F & SAT 9:30–8, SUN 9:30–6.

This is Chicago's best-known German deli, located in the heart of the German populated area northwest of the Loop. Once inside, you'll figure out why. Rows of German, Hungarian and Austrian wines and liquors line the first row of the store which leads you back to the butcher case, where you'll find yourself indecisive over which sausage to choose. It's sausage heaven. Blutwurst, thuringer, onion sausage, fleishwurst and the list goes on. Homemade German potato salad can't be disregarded and you must begin with a bit of herring salad. The Old World ambience continues with a line of pumpernickel and rye breads, imported jams and preserves, coffees and teas, imported sweets and a few refrigerated tortes to finish off the meal in style. But don't let the Old World mood deceive you. Kuhn's is one of the few delis to offer completely modern nitrite-free franks and bacon.

MEYER IMPORT DELICATESSEN

3306 North Lincoln Avenue, Chicago 60657. Telephone 281-8979. Hours: M–F 9:30–8, SAT 9–7, SUN 11–6.

Just north of Kuhn's is another worthy stop on any German cook's shopping spree. Meyer Import is not quite as spacious as its neighbor, but one suspects it carries just about the same number of items, stashed in corners and stacked to the ceiling. It's almost hard to move around. Shelves of wines and beers from all countries, liqueurs from Germany and Austria, a refrigerated caseful of Continental pastries, and imported preserves, relishes, and canned vegetables line the shelves. But it's the sausage that brings customers back again and again, from the large franks to the dark-colored blood sausage, from the mettwurst to the thuringer. More than likely, you'll hear German spoken here as the friendly staff waits on neighborhood shoppers.

Greek

Just west of the Loop is what everyone refers to as old Greektown, a four-block strip along Halsted Street that includes bakeries, groceries and plenty of Greek restaurants, which pull in customers, even from the suburbs, despite the neighborhood's scroungy appearance. But like so many ethnic groups, the Greeks are moving throughout Chicago. Many of them have opened businesses on or near the North Side's Lawrence Avenue, which is becoming known as Chicago's second Greektown.

ATHENS GROCERY
324 South Halsted Street, Chicago 60606. Telephone 332-6737 or 454-0940. Hours: M–SAT 8–8, SUN 8–2.

While Greektown's down-and-out residents may be picking up cans of beans from the small selection of regular groceries, well-heeled shoppers, perhaps planning a Greek dinner party, can be seen picking up wheels of one of three kinds of feta cheese, kasseri cheese, Greek olives in brine and bottles of retsina, that wine that only true Greek aficionados can love. Jars of grape leaves, a whole row of pasta imported from Greece and prepared marinated salads also tempt. A trip next door to the Pan Hellenic Bakery (see Baked Goods) produces fine dinner-party desserts.

WEST MEAT MARKET
2549 West Lawrence Avenue, Chicago 60625. Telephone 769-4956 or 769-4957. Hours: M–SAT 9–9, SUN 10–4.

This is much more than a meat market. If you are into Greek cooking, this clean, spacious shop is a must to visit not only for its high-quality legs of lamb and cuts of beef, but for the several varieties of Greek olives, cheeses, oils, spices and other Mediterranean goodies. It is one of a very few high-quality Greek markets in the city. Also a nice but small selection of produce and everyday grocery items is offered.

Indian & Pakistani

INDIA GROCERS
5010 North Sheridan Road, Chicago 60640. Telephone 334-3351. Hours: M–SUN 10–7.

When Chicago's better Indian restaurants need the exotic seasonings and spices that make that cuisine so very special, they turn to India Grocers. The store is a bazaar of spices, whole and ground, all kinds of beans, whole, split or ground, rice and other grains. Pickles and chutneys, fresh Oriental vegetables and Indian cookbooks are all part of the wares. Shoppers can purchase by bulk, or in smaller quantity, depending upon need.

INDIA INTERNATIONAL
2537 West Devon Avenue, Chicago 60659. Telephone 465-8382. Hours: W–M 11–8.

A tiny shop located on Devon Avenue where shoppers mix from many ethnic cultures—Pakistani, Indian, Jewish and Oriental. India International is perhaps the smallest of three Indian food markets in a one-block area, but it is clean and has orderly rows of packaged dals—those dried beans, peas and lentils so important in Indian cuisine. Spices and nuts and seeds are reasonably priced compared to supermarket versions. You can also find Indian flatbreads such as pappadams, rice in bulk, and canned foods such as assorted pickles, chutneys and mango juice and pulp.

PATEL BROTHERS
2542 West Devon Avenue, Chicago 60659. Telephone 764-1857 or 764-1858. Hours: W–M 10:30–8.
2034 West Devon Avenue, Chicago 60659. Telephone 764-1853. Hours: W–M 10–8.
1631 Oakton Place, Des Plaines 60018. Telephone 635-8413. Hours: W–SUN 11–5, M 11–8.

The Devon Avenue shops are bright and small and contain all the ingredients for classic Indian cooking including bulk basmati, extra-long, or Uncle Ben's rice, dals (dried lentils, beans), flours and spices. These shops and the branch in Des Plaines are part of a national chain of Indian groceries based in Houston.

JAINSON INTERNATIONAL
2540 West Devon Avenue, Chicago 60659. Telephone 262-3500. Hours: W–M 11–8.

Even for cooks not interested in preparing Indian dishes, this is a good spot to stock up on cinnamon sticks, rice, cloves and nuts in bulk, because prices are better than supermarket prices. Durum flour, mango pulp, dried apricots and dates can be found here as well as dals, pickles and more.

OTHER INDIAN SOURCES

GUJRAT GROCERS
2606 West Devon Avenue, Chicago 60659. Telephone 465-2206. Hours: 11–8 daily.

KAMDAR IMPORTS
5024 North Broadway Avenue, Chicago 60640. Telephone 878-2525 or 878-2526. Hours: W–SUN 11–7:30.

KAVITHA IMPORTS
4826 North Sheridan Road, Chicago 60640. Telephone 784-5554. Hours: 10–8 daily.

SANGAM
2050 West Devon Avenue, Chicago 60648. Telephone 262-6222. Hours: 10:30–8 daily.
630 North Addison Road, Villa Park 60181. Telephone 530-7341. Hours: M–SAT 10:30–8, SUN noon–8.

SONA
423 North Bolingbrook Drive, Bolingbrook 60439. Telephone 759-3689. Hours: 11–8 daily.

Italian

See also Falbo's and Pomodor Gelateria in the cheese section of Dairy Products and Caputo's Food Market in the Produce chapter.

CONTE DI SAVOIA
Jeffro Plaza, 555 West Roosevelt Road, Chicago 60607. Telephone 666-3471. Hours: M–SAT 9–6, SUN 9–4. Customers may sign up at store to be put on mailing list.

Long before anyone was called a "gourmet cook," before boutique groceries and an interest in ethnic cooking styles, back in that long-ago time there was Conte di Savoia. The store goes back half a century or more and is named after the ship that carried its founder to the United States from Italy. Conte di Savoia still has its roots in its Italian homeland, its shelves alive with all the comestibles needed in an Italian kitchen: extra virgin olive oils, imported dried pastas, espresso beans and grinds, polenta mixes, and much more. But, today, Conte di Savoia offers a more international selection than its original inventory. There are spices in bulk from the Orient, seasonings from Indonesia for sambals, tahini and falafel mixes from the Middle East, dried herbs and spices, couscous, chutneys and curry powders. The store is brightly lit, almost like a quick mart in its initial appearance. But, there is a verisimilitude at work here. A quick walk through the aisles reveals what Conte di Savoia is all about.

CONVITO ITALIANO
Plaza del Lago, 1515 Sheridan Road, Wilmette 60091. Telephone 251-3654.
Hours: M–F 10–7, SAT 10–5:30.
CONVITO ITALIANO CHESTNUT GALLERIA
11 East Chestnut, Chicago 60611. Telephone 943-2983. Hours: M–F 10–8:30,
SAT 9:30–5:30.

To list what Convito Italiano stocks is hardly to do justice to this innovative emporium. Yes, they stock the special Italian and other European items to be expected of a fine food store. And, their prepared selections are uniformly delicious whether a frozen sauce or dishes such as osso bucco or fresh pastas, salads, breads and other bakery goods in abundant array. The cheeses alone are an Italian education. The inventory goes far beyond Parmesan, romano and others that have become near clichés of the Italian cheese larder. Try scamorze or the fresh curds of mascarpone from among choices available from time to time. The wine department is not only well stocked, but service people know their wares. Thus, if you need something rare and special, they'll be able to find the right bottle for you. This is probably the deepest inventory of Italian wines in any specialty shop in and around Chicago. The takeout menus abound with riches. They'll put together something as light as a simple picnic spread for two or as elaborate as a multicourse Italian feast for whatever number you name. Staff party planners specialize in detail work to make your event successful. Both stores (in Wilmette, the first location, and in the Chestnut Galleria) are delights in which to shop and taste. Each is bright and airy with a kitchen freshness in the way foods are stored, showcased and sold. In addition to the grocery, wine and prepared-food sections, each store has a sit-down restaurant for lunch or dinner meals. The same high standards apply.

To be placed on their mail- order catalog list (notification of wine tastings, special cooking demonstrations, etc.) call or write either store.

D'ANDREA & SON
Cermak Plaza, 7055 West Cermak, Berwyn 60402. Telephone 484-8121. Hours:
M–F 9:30–6, SAT 9:30–5, SUN 10–1.

The D'Andrea family has been involved in the food business for over forty years and in its present location since 1967. The decades of experience make this more than just another food store. The six thousand square feet of retail selling space contain merchandise in five basic categories: groceries, deli items, kitchen equipment, baked goods and wines. The groceries include a dozen brands of imported and domestic pasta, fifteen brands of canned tomatoes and tomato products, twenty brands of olive and other vegetable oils, a variety of spices, a forty-eight-foot section of vinegars, canned and glassed fish products, vegetable goods, soups and so forth. Deli selections include Italian luncheon meats, cheeses, salads, sandwiches and freshly made sausage and roasted beef. The sausage is made daily in-house from 100 percent pork and contains no water, chemicals or preservatives. You will also find a choice of spaghetti sauces cooked on the premises, and a selection of pastas, including ravioli. A small housewares section holds noodle makers, pasta machines, dishes, bowls and assorted gadgets. The D'Andrea & Son bakery produces a variety of pizzas and Italian breads, the old-fashioned crusty kind without preservatives. The wine department stocks a good selection of Italian imports, most moderately priced, plus some California jug wines.

GINO'S ITALIAN IMPORTS
3420–22 North Harlem Avenue, Chicago 60635. Telephone 745-8310 or 745-8311. Hours: M–F 9–7, SAT–SUN 8–4.

Harlem Avenue is the avenue of pasta, Italian sausage and olive oil. When the Italians began moving from their old Taylor and Oakley Street addresses they headed for northwest Chicago and close-by suburbs. Now one can find many more Italian food shops along a three- or four-mile stretch of Harlem than in the old neighborhood. One of the newest is Gino's, where neat-as-a-pin shelves house the typical imported pastas, oils, vinegars and packaged cookies. But Gino's is known primarily for its fine homemade sausages, especially the Calabrese sausage, and for its prime veal from Provimi. Some cookware, gifts and dishware are also offered. If fresh pasta is in order, pop into The Pasta Shoppe next door (see listing).

GRAN SASSO
260 Green Bay Road, Highwood 60040. Telephone 433-1131. Hours: M–SAT 9–6.

This tiny store is not nearly as large as the central Italian mountain range for which it is named. But, within its small confines will be found assorted packaged breads, plus imported biscuits and cookies, cooking accessories, condiments, dried pastas and boxed or canned goods from Italy. Refrigerated counters hold rounds or bricks of cheese and Italian meats. Boned baccalà (codfish) is one of the store's most popular selections. There's a good choice of marinated olives—Greek, Sicilian and Italian—each with its own flavor and character. Mushrooms abound: marinated for salads, or dried for use in cooking. And if Perrier is too passé, there is a selection of bottled still and sparkling waters from Italy.

L'APPETITO IMPORTED ITALIAN FOODS
30 East Huron Street, Chicago 60611. Telephone 787-9881. Hours: M–SAT 10–6.

Tucked away in an unlikely high-rise corner near Michigan Avenue, this tiny shop carries a nice selection of Italian cheeses, sausages, fresh pasta and wonderful takeout submarine sandwiches on ten-inch buns at reasonable prices. It also offers a complete line of dried pastas, oils, chocolates and some equipment from Italy. The cheese selection emphasizes the soft variety such as robiola, caprino and buffalo mozzarella.

JOSEPH FOOD MART
8235 West Irving Park Road, Chicago 60634. Telephone 625-0118. Hours: TU–SAT 9–7, SUN 9–3.

This family-run shop carries a line of complete Italian foods from deli items, fresh meats (including baby goat during holiday season), fish, produce and canned and packaged items. Homemade Italian sausage is a specialty. Joseph is one of the largest Italian markets on the west side. Dried pastas include Agnesi, De Cecco and Divella brands. Olives, beans and grains are in bins. Perugina chocolates and holiday cakes such as pandoro and panetone are also available. The shop is only five minutes from O'Hare Airport—worth a quick taxi ride for anyone on a layover.

NOTTOLI SAUSAGE SHOP
5027 North Harlem Avenue, Chicago 60656. Telephone 631-0662. Hours: M–SAT 9–6, SUN 9–3.

Perhaps not as impressive as larger shops on Harlem, Nottoli's still carries a complete line of packaged goods, cheeses, sausages made on premises and other meats.

PASTA FACTORY
3141 Kirchoff Road, Rolling Meadows 60007. Telephone 398-6195. Hours: M–F 9:30–6:30, SAT 9–6.

Fresh pasta is the specialty here. Choices include egg pasta made in the traditional way with semolina and durum flours, or those made with spinach or tomato or parsley and garlic for color and flavor accents. Stuffed shells are sold frozen and include tortellini, gnocchi and cavetelli. Even German-style spaetzle is available. Pasta Factory also features a line of twenty-two sauces, plus ready-to-bake dinner-size portions of lasagna, ravioli, manicotti and the like. In addition to its retail business, the store supplies several well-known food service operations with fresh pastas.

THE PASTA SHOPPE
3418 North Harlem Avenue, Chicago 60635. Telephone 889-4300. Hours: M–SAT 9–6, SUN 9:30–2.

This tiny shop features high-quality fresh pasta and a few sauces. A picture-window view of the back room, where all the pasta is made, makes waiting for an order fun as you watch the long strands of noodles emerging from the large pasta machines. Meat- and cheese-filled ravioli and tortellini come in plain egg pasta or spinach or tomato flavors. Also available on a daily basis are an assortment of flat noodles from linguini to fettuccine.

PASTA SUGO
2852 Broadway, Chicago 60657. Telephone 327-8866. Hours: M–TH, SAT 10–8, F 10–9, SUN 11–7. Mailing list by request.

Fresh pastas and sauces are the featured items in this store that wholesales to several major restaurants, but also sells to individual customers across the retail counter. *Sugo* is Italian for sauce and they make ten varieties, ready to go, complementing the fresh noodles and other pastas. If you are unfamiliar with any of the sauces, just ask for a taste. Try their version of pesto alla genovese made with fresh basil, garlic, pignolia nuts, virgin olive oil and imported parmesan. In addition to the pasta and sauces, you'll find various Italian sandwiches, even a version of the Philly steak. For party orders, they have free delivery, a rare convenience among Chicago food stores.

PASTAFICIO

122 Highwood Avenue, Highwood 60040. Telephone 432-5459. Hours: TU–SAT 9–5. Mailing list on request.

Fresh and dry pastas, Italian sauces, frozen entrees and side dishes, as well as a variety of prepared Italian condiments and other items are the stock in trade of this handsome store. The bright and white decor, almost high-tech, showcases food-stuffs ranging from angel hair pastas, basil fettuccine, tortellacci with meat and cream sauces as well as a host of other choices. A printed brochure gives mouth-watering descriptions, such as this for a pomodoro sauce: "whole ripe tomatoes, fresh onions, butter and the finest herbs and spices, simmered. . . ." Well, you get the idea. The staff at Pastaficio can be especially helpful if you are planning a full dinner or dinner party, and they will even do the catering if need be.

REX IMPORTED ITALIAN FOODS AND LIQUORS

5045 North Harlem Avenue, Chicago 60656. Telephone 763-5175. Hours: M–SAT 9–6:30, SUN 9–5.

From the gallon tins of olive oil to the rows of imported pastas, this is one of the most complete of the Harlem Avenue Italian shops. Prosciutto and large wheels of bel paese cheese line one wall and the back offers a butcher counter with several varieties of homemade sausage and pork, veal and beef cuts. Some fresh ravioli and other pastas are sold as well as sauces. The store is twenty-five years old, and Tony Spartara has owned it for eleven years.

RIVIERA ITALIAN IMPORTED FOODS

3220 North Harlem Avenue, Chicago 60634. Telephone 637-4252. Hours: M–F 9–6, SAT 8–6, SUN 8–3.

Riviera Market is a large neighborhood operation with a stock that runs the gamut from imported gourmet foods to Italian novelty gadgets. Italian salamis, prosciutto, espresso coffees, cheeses and pastas are just a few of the items bounti-fully stocked. In addition, cooks will find a wide array of herbs, seasonings and legumes, pasta machines and Italian ceramic dishes.

Japanese

STAR MARKET
3349 North Clark Street, Chicago 60657. Telephone 472-0599, 472-2184. Hours: M–SAT 9–7, SUN 10–3.

Here is where the Japanese community shops. The Star Market carries the freshest of produce, from seaweeds you've never seen before to shiitake mushrooms and fresh greens. Japanese cooks buy fish here for their sushi and sashimi. Gorgeous fresh tuna, conch, squid, shrimp and crab line the case; their low price usually can't be matched even by large fish markets in town. Once you've got the vegetables and seafood, turn to the shelves loaded with Japanese and Chinese canned products of all kinds from wasabi (that hot green horseradish condiment that goes so well with sushi) to soy sauce. You're bound to leave with more than you bargained for, but that's half the fun.

YENCHING ORIENTAL GROCERY STORE
6421 North Western Avenue, Chicago 60645. Telephone 465-7999. Hours: 10–7 daily.

This neat shop carries Japanese packaged foods plus fresh fish and produce and some other packaged Oriental foods such as Chinese sauces. Live crabs in season.

Korean

ORIENTAL MARKET
5131 North Western Avenue, Chicago 60625. Telephone 989-7811. Hours: SUN–TH 10–9, F–SAT 10–10.

A former gas station has been converted to a well-stocked, clean Korean food market which is run by friendly Byung Ho Park. Ask a question and the staff will willingly help. Produce is fresh looking and includes several kinds of fresh seaweed, not a common item in Chicago. Tofu and tofu products, frozen prepared dumplings and other frozen foods, rows of canned and bottled foods and sauces, and a nice selection of frozen whole fish, including flounder and giant squid, round out the selection.

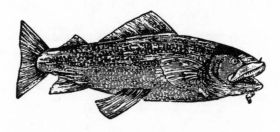

Latin

LA GUADALUPANA
3215 West 26th Street, Chicago 60623. Telephone 847-3191. Hours: SUN–F 8–8, SAT 8–9.

A full-fledged grocery store that carries Mexican products, produce and meats, this shop is a good source for fresh masa, the treated, ground corn that's used for making tortillas and tamales. If you have never made tortillas, you're in for a surprise. The fresh masa results in a much fuller, more corn-flavored tortilla than most commercial products. And it's much easier to work with than starting with a dry masa harina mix. The masa also comes flavored with peppers, if you like your tortillas hot, and in a coarser version for making tamales.

LA PLAZA
1449 West Irving Park Road, Chicago 60613. Telephone 528-8680. Hours: M–SAT 9–9, SUN 10–6.

A good source for an assortment of Mexican and South American food products from tortillas and chilies to canned and packaged goods. Produce such as plantains, dried banana leaves and chili peppers, plus a good selection of Mexican-style meats are offered.

LA UNICA FOOD MART
1515 West Devon Avenue, Chicago 60660. Telephone 274-7788. Hours: M–SAT 9–9, SUN 9–4.

One of the city's most complete lines of Latin American specialties is found here, including packaged products from Colombia, Venezuela, Argentina, Brazil, Mexico, Puerto Rico and Spain. Fresh meat is cut to customer's order. In-season tropical fruits are also found here as well as a good assortment of dried chilies. Before buying any ingredients, shoppers can stop by a small cafeteria in the back of the store to sample from some of the following Latin specialties: plantains, Cuban-style tamales, yellow chicken with rice, and flan.

TRUJILLO CARNICERIA
3300 West 26th Street, Chicago 60623. Telephone 277-0686. Hours: M–SUN 8–9.

This clean, small supermarket/butcher shop is located on 26th Street, which has become one of the bustling commercial areas of the Mexican-American population in Chicago. Here you can find most ingredients for Mexican dishes including fresh chorizo, dried and fresh chilies, imported canned goods, pumpkin seeds and fried pork rinds.

Middle Eastern

MIDDLE EASTERN BAKERY & GROCERY
*1512 West Foster Avenue, Chicago 60640. Telephone 561-2224. Hours: M–F
9–9, SUN 9–5.*

Pita bread is baked daily in this wholesale and retail store near Andersonville,
the old Swedish neighborhood that is slowly giving way to an influx of Oriental
and Middle Eastern residents. In addition to the bread and a small selection of
honey-coated and nut pastries, you can find one of the area's largest selections of
dried beans, grains, lentils and peas. A browse through the shelves will also turn
up imported foods from Jordan, Syria, Egypt and other Middle Eastern countries:
dried sour cherries, large bags of dried mint, rose and orange water, three brands
of couscous, tahini (a peanut butter-like mixture that goes into the dip called hum-
mus), teas and more. Prices on bulk items are very reasonable.

PALESTINE BAKERY
2639 West 63rd Street, Chicago 60629. Telephone 925-5978. Hours: 8–10 daily.

A small selection of baked goods including pita bread baked on premises, plus
cheeses, olive oils and other canned ingredients.

MIDDLE EAST TRADING
*2636 West Devon Avenue, Chicago 60659. Telephone 262-2848. Hours: SUN–TH
8–9, F–SAT 8–10.*

This tiny shop features foods as well as tapes, records and knick-knacks from
the Middle East. Some Bulgarian cheese, Turkish halvah, chickpeas, rice in large
bags, and pita bread are sold here.

Philippine

PHILHOUSE CORPORATION
5430 North Clark Street, Chicago 60640. Telephone 784-1176. Hours: 9–8 daily.

Fine produce marks this tidy market with its neat rows of canned Philippine products such as coconut balls in syrup, packaged noodles, fresh and frozen fish, including live crabs in season. Many basic Oriental products can be found here, too. The produce includes a very fresh array of chayotes, plantains, lemon grass, tamarind and strange-looking squashes.

R. C. PHILIPPINE TRADING CORP.
1132–34 West Fulton Market, Chicago 60607. Telephone 829-1600 or 829-1601. Hours: M–F 8:30–6, SAT 7–4.

This large market is also a wholesale distributor of Oriental foods, so you'll find more than just Philippine products here. Located in an old warehouse in one of Chicago's wholesale districts near the Randolph Street Market, this is a busy store, packed on Saturdays by those in the Philippine community picking up their weekly supplies. You'll see few outsiders. But it's certainly worth the trip to see such exotic items as grated cassava and obe, yucca, banana leaves, and species of frozen fish you've never heard of. If you like rice you can buy fifty-pound sacks of it here. But you can also stock up on soy sauce, all kinds of Chinese noodles, long beans and coconut milk.

Polish

CAESAR'S POLISH DELI
901 North Damen Avenue, Chicago 60622. Telephone 486-6190. Hours: M–F 9–6, SAT 9–4.

The smell of meat and cabbage cooking greets visitors to this old Polish neighborhood grocery store/deli where you can find excellent pierogi (those dumplings that are so good filled with cheese, cabbage, mushrooms or meat, and fried in butter), home-style beef rolls stuffed with vegetables, and wonderful aromatic homemade soups like czarina, tomato and rice, barley and zurek, or a white borscht. Before you know it, you'll have picked up a whole dinner to go from the hardworking Polish cooks behind the counter.

KASIA'S POLISH DELI
2101 West Chicago Avenue, Chicago 60622. Telephone 486-6163. Hours: M–SAT 9–6, SUN 12–5.

In the mood for hearty food? Kasia's is the place to go for a hearty takeout meal.

Choose from special pork tips offered one day or braised Polish sausages another, and team them with homemade potato or cucumber salads, plum, blueberry or cabbage pierogis, filling beet or mushroom barley soups, and all kinds of cheese or fruit-filled blintzes for dessert. Friendly service.

Swedish

ERICKSON'S DELICATESSEN & FISH MARKET
5250 North Clark Street, Chicago 60640. Telephone 561-5634. Hours: M–W 10–5, TH–SAT 9–5, SUN 10–4.

This tiny storefront is located in Andersonville, Chicago's Swedish neighborhood on the North Side. While the Scandinavians have been moving out of the neighborhood and Orientals moving in, there is still a core of shops catering to Scandinavian tastes. Erickson's tiny fish case offers some fresh selections, but the majority of space is set aside for the smoked fish so prized by the Scandinavians, plus their luftfisk, a dried cod with a strong flavor which may take some getting used to. The few prepared dishes include Swedish meatballs and rice pudding.

WIKSTROM SCANDINAVIAN AMERICAN GOURMET FOODS
5247 North Clark Street, Chicago 60640. Telephone 878-0601. Hours: M–SAT 9–6, SUN 11–3.

Ingvar Wikstrom likes to let customers browse in his ten-year-old Andersonville shop while sipping a complimentary cup of Swedish coffee. It's a good idea, because it takes a while to choose from his assortment of Swedish prepared foods. His friendly reputation travels, it seems, because many of his customers are from out of town. You'll find here, prepared daily, the famous Scandinavian dishes like brown beans, pickled herring, Swedish meatballs, smoked liver sausage and rice pudding. To go with the Norwegian smoked salmon and gravlax, Wikstrom's tangy mustard dill sauce fits the bill. Cans and jars of imported products such as tart lingnonberries and smoked fish line the store's shelves and, in case customers get tired, they can relax at the few tables in the front.

Thai & Vietnamese

The cooking of Thailand has invaded Chicago. A growing Thai population has enriched the city with more than forty restaurants where Chicagoans have learned to enjoy Thai dishes. Many cooks are game enough to try cooking at home such exotic dishes as pad thai and satay.

The place to go for Thai ingredients is Argyle Street on the city's North Side. Within a two-block walk in this rather run-down neighborhood, you'll find a dozen shops carrying the coconut milk, noc-nam (fish sauce), fresh coriander, tamarind paste, hot chilies and all of the other exotic ingredients for one of the world's spiciest cuisines.

Although not in the same abundance as the Thai shops, Vietnamese markets have opened on Argyle, but most of the stores carry items for both cuisines. Here is a brief, selective listing of shops on Argyle, plus a few in other locations.

HAI GROCERY, INC.
5014 North Broadway Avenue, Chicago 60640. Telephone 561-5345. Hours: F–W 10–8.

Fresh produce and seafood greet shoppers entering this small but clean store that's been in operation since 1974: fresh clams, fish, lemon grass, Thai eggplant, mint, basil and cilantro. The usual lineup of canned goods and noodles supplements the fresh foods. Friendly service.

HOA-AN CO.
1131 West Argyle Street, Chicago 60640. Telephone 275-4643. Hours: 9–7:30 daily.

The cleanest shop within two blocks, although small. It carries a selection of herbs as well as Chinese, Thai, Philippine and Vietnamese packaged foods.

HOA NAM
1101–3 West Argyle Street, Chicago 60640. Telephone 275-9157. Hours: M 9–7, SAT 9–8.

One of the largest shops on the street with a good selection of fresh produce, including bitter melon and Chinese long beans. Chinese, Thai, Vietnamese and other Oriental packaged foods are offered as well.

THAI ORIENTAL MARKET
1656 East 55th Street, Chicago 60615. Telephone 324-8714. Hours: M–SAT 9–7, SUN 9–5.

Although this is another typically small Oriental grocery, the fact that it is located in Hyde Park near the South Side makes it a rarity. Packaged noodles, curry pastes and thousand-year-old duck eggs are offered, as well as Oriental canned goods.

VAN HOA GROCERY
1028 West Argyle Street, Chicago 60640. Telephone 989-7850. Hours: M–F 9:30–7, SAT–SUN 9–8.

One of the smaller shops, but the friendly owner makes up for the lack of size. A typical array of Chinese, Japanese and some Cambodian packaged foods.

Fish

Time was if you wanted fresh fish in and around Chicago, you usually got something called "whitefish" or "lakefish" or some other meaningless generic designation. Lake Michigan perch, smelts and coho were about the only real alternatives to frozen fish in the local supermarket. Now widespread jet transport has made Chicago a virtual seaport, bringing to our specialty fish shops denizens of the deep from Atlantic, Pacific and Caribbean waters, not to mention other finned delights from far-off fishing fleets.

As Ben Franklin reminded us more than two centuries ago, fish, like guests, begin to stink after three days. So, it's not so odd that we don't want our fish to smell or taste too fishy! When shopping, look for fish that is still firm of flesh, with bright, rather than dull eyes; the gills should always be bright red. And, of course, the smell should be mild.

The many specialty fish stores in and around Chicago not only bring us fresh products, but many also sell special cookware and kitchen or barbeque equipment to make the job of preparation a bit easier. Even without special equipment, generally most soft fish should be cooked not much more than six to seven minutes, if sautéed or grilled, and no more than ten to eleven minutes, if baked. The fish house where you shop regularly will be able to give you specific tips and cooking instructions. In fact, a fishmonger can be one of the most valuable culinary friends to cultivate when you are shopping for absolutely the best of his products.

Japanese markets are also excellent sources for fresh fish; see Star Market and Yenching Oriental Grocery Store in the Ethnic Foods chapter.

ANNABELLE'S FISH MARKET
2375 South Arlington Heights Road, Arlington Heights 60005. Telephone 439-1028.
Edens Plaza, 1108 Skokie Boulevard, Wilmette 60081. Telephone 256- 0110.
Hours: M–TH 11–7, F–SAT 11–9, SUN noon–5. Mailings provide latest information on products, recipes, etc. Sign up in market.

Annabelle's is one of those fairly new ventures that combine retail counter trade with a restaurant. Both sides of the business benefit from the array of fresh seafood flown in daily from major ports. The market stocks at least twenty-five varieties of soft fish, including virtually anything you might need to make sushi and sashimi. Not only do they have the fish for sushi, but all the condiments and equipment: nori (seaweed), wasabi, pink ginger root and bamboo rollers. For other cooking needs, the shop stocks shallot sauce for oysters, shrimp cocktail sauce and vinaigrette dressings. Freshly made chowders are also available.

BURHOP'S
One Fish Plaza, 745 North LaSalle, Chicago 60610. Telephone 642-9600.
Cove Plaza, 418 West 22nd Street, Lombard 60148. Telephone 932-1030.
Plaza del Lago, 1515 North Sheridan Road, Wilmette 60091. Telephone 256-6400.
1413 Waukegan Road, Glenview 60025. Telephone 998-1770.
187 Skokie Valley Highway, Highland Park 60035. Telephone 831-0100.
Hours: MON noon–6, TU–TH 10–6, F–SAT 9–6; Chicago store open until 7 p.m.

Burhop's has been synonymous with fresh seafood in Chicago for decades. Now it is a much more sophisticated operation than in those days when "Pops" Burhop would be behind the counter cutting roundfish for the walk-in trade. But that attention to detail and freshness still is being carried on at the company's several retail shops. Most spectacular is the large market at One Fish Plaza which features not only fresh fish and shellfish, but all the gadgets and paraphernalia good cooks need to be well equipped when going nautical. Wines and prepared foods are also a part of the inventory.

CAROLYN COLLINS CAVIAR
PO Box 662, Crystal Lake 60014. Telephone (815) 459-6210. Mail order only. To get on the mailing list just write or telephone.

In the spirit of American entrepreneurship, Carolyn Collins went from raising Siberian huskies to marketing domestic caviars. After the Iranian revolution, when Baltic Sea caviar skyrocketed in price, Collins devoted herself to discovering those domestic roes that could serve not only as less expensive replacements, but could stand on their own merits. Thus golden trout roe, small beads of salmon roe and, of course, sturgeon roe from Washington State's Columbia River are staples of her specialized inventory. Recently, the company has begun offering by direct mail an occasional specialty ingredient that may have nothing to do with caviar, per se, but showcases the diversity of the American cuisine. For example, when Appalachian ramps are available, Collins distributes them through the retail outlets that stock her other wares.

CHICAGO FISH HOUSE
1250 West Division Street, Chicago 60622. Telephone 227-7000. Hours: M–F 9–6, SAT 8–4.

The Midwest's largest wholesale fish market also has a retail store attached that has a fine selection of seafood, seafood accompaniments, including wines and sauces, cookbooks, and a small demonstration area where a resident cooking teacher or guest chefs clarify the mysteries of fish cookery every Saturday. It's clean, it's fun, and although the prices aren't the lowest in the city, you can count on the fish being fresh. The Fish House is located just off the Kennedy Expressway northwest of the Loop.

DICOLA'S SEAFOOD
10754 South Western Avenue, Chicago 60643. Telephone 238-7071. Hours: M–TH 9–9:30; F 9–10; SAT 9–9:30.

Although Dicola's sells fresh fish, what the crowds line up for on Saturdays is the breaded and fried seafood, from catfish to smelt and shrimp. The staff is busy cooking up orders to go in the front of the shop. Customers also can buy seafood that's coated with batter and ready to be cooked at home. The breaded fish is on display in a case that's larger than the fresh fish case in the rear of the store. The fresh selection includes white bass, snapper, sole, trout and more. Prices are very reasonable.

HAGEN'S FISH MARKET
5635 West Montrose Avenue, Chicago 60634. Telephone 283-1944. Hours: M–TH 8–10, F–SAT 8–midnight, SUN 11–8.

Since 1946, Hagen's has been hot-smoking fish in the same delectable way, by soaking fish in brine and then letting it hang over smoldering hardwoods. Owners Don and Charlene Breede will clean and smoke the catch of sports fishermen too. In addition to the smoked chubs, salmon, trout, sturgeon and eel, you can also pick up fresh fish, shrimp and lobster at good prices. Although it's not convenient to downtowners, the shop is open long after most fish markets have shuttered for the day.

ISAACSON & STEIN FISH COMPANY
800 West Fulton Street, Chicago 60607. Telephone 421-2444. Hours: M–F 6:30–5:15, SAT 6:30–3:30.

Be prepared to elbow your way through this busy fish market on a Saturday morning. This is where many of the city's Orientals do their fish shopping and they're a discriminating bunch when it comes to fresh seafood. Attractive open bins of fish on ice include the usual lineup of sole, snapper and whitefish as well as catfish, buffalo fish and kingfish, squid, octopus and many more. This is basically a warehouse and the floors are dripping with melted ice, so wear your boots.

LINCOLN FISH HOUSE
5300 North Lincoln Avenue, Chicago 60625. Telephone 561-3445. Hours: M–TH 9–9, F–SAT 9–11.

Formerly called Berwyn Fisheries, this shop carries reasonably priced seafood and smoked-on-the-premises fish. The new owners stock a small selection that often will include giant squid and octopus, as well as the more familiar whitefish and trout.

PICK FISHERIES
702 West Fulton Street, Chicago 60607. Telephone 226-4700. Hours: M–F 6–4:30, SAT 6–1.

One block away from its neighbor across the freeway, Isaacson & Stein, the smaller Pick Fisheries is worth checking out for better prices, although the fish doesn't always look as fresh. The firm also carries a wide range of caviars.

Gourmet & Takeout Foods

Chicago has seen a tremendous growth of gourmet and upscale takeout food shops in the last five years. It comes as no surprise that the increasing number of families with two working parents or single parents who work full time has had a major impact on the food business.

Quick meals are a must, whether that means hamburgers from McDonalds, frozen entrees from the supermarket or freshly prepared foods from a neighborhood gourmet shop. All seem to be booming. As the need for fast, quality food was recognized, more caterers, restaurateurs and even supermarket operators have opened stores or departments that offer hot and cold, high-quality foods from pâtés to fruit tarts, from deli meats to whole roasted turkey, veal or beef. Most of the shops are flourishing on or near North Michigan Avenue or on the North Shore where affluent singles and working families can afford to buy takeout foods.

Marshall Field was one of the first to offer special imported foods and takeout salads in its State Street store. Field's gourmet food department is due for a facelift soon, but in the meantime newer, smaller shops have popped up offering more innovative fare. Convito Italiano, Zambrana's, Neiman-Marcus and others have proven that good marketing, modern facilities and attractive displays sell as well as innovative, fresh foods.

Check the Ethnic Foods chapter for other sources of takeout foods, such as New Quan Wah and Phoenix Company Bakery for Chinese, Kuhn's Delicatessen for German, Convito Italiano for Italian, Caesar and Kasia's delis for Polish, and Wickstrom for Swedish. Many shops in the Baked Goods section also have takeout, such as Cafe Bennison and Maison Barusseau. And for Italian foods to go, see Pomodoro Gelateria in the cheese section of Dairy Products.

A LA CARTE
*111 Greenbay Road, Wilmette 60091. Telephone 256-4102. Hours: M–F 10–7,
SAT 10–5:30. Mailing list by request.*

A la Carte is a gourmet kitchen for the busy professional who doesn't have the time to cook. It is familiar food, not intimidating. Yet the listings of what can be available appears almost limitless, ranging from soups and salads to entrees, appetizers and desserts. They will prepare for an individual or a large party. And when it comes to catering, they'll do all the preparations, bring food to your party location, provide serving platters and set up everything for serving, all at an average cost of around $8 a person.

AN APPLE A DAY
*691 Vernon Avenue, Glencoe 60022. Telephone 835-2620. Hours: TU–SAT
7:30–8; although not open to walk-in customers on Monday, they will deliver.*

Just like a small country store, An Apple a Day welcomes customers with its bright red front door and cheery decor. An old-fashioned apple press, baskets of bright red flowers, polished wood floors, intricately patterned green wallpaper and brass ceiling fans on a red ceiling combine to create the shop's homespun atmosphere. Their food selection includes fresh pies and tarts (try Shaker lemon), muffins and other baked goods. To quench a thirst there is hot cider in the winter and chilled juices in warmer months. And, if you are a commuter on the go, they'll put together a tasty box lunch on request, or a country breakfast of rolls and coffee. They have free delivery service, too.

BEAUTIFUL FOODS
*546 Chestnut Street, Winnetka 60093. Telephone 440-4066. Hours: M–F
9:30–5:30, SAT 8–5.*

An open glass-enclosed kitchen is the heart of Beautiful Foods. Here, shoppers can see the team of cooks rolling out doughs, mixing sauces, finishing the soups and dinners that have proven so popular with taste-conscious customers. The kitchen's marble countertops and Mediterranean tiled flooring are also found in the retail area. Wares include frozen sauces and prepared dinners to take out, jars of chutneys, preserves, jams and fruits. If you cannot wait for the Vidalia onion season, try a bottle of the preserved Vidalias. Lavash, French breads, crackers and biscuits are among baked goods, and there is a selection of fresh pasta. Inside the refrigerated cases are salads and marinated vegetables, cheeses and meats. The store also has a small cafe/restaurant where lunches and dinners are served from a daily menu of freshly made foods.

CITY MARKET
2828 North Clark Street, Chicago 60657. Telephone 525-9072. Hours: M–F 10:30–9, SAT 10:30–7, SUN 11–6. Free one-hour parking in adjacent garage.

What used to be a grand old palace of a movie theater was gutted some years ago, except for its ornate terra cotta exterior, and transformed into a multi-tiered shopping center. On the lowest level of the center, away from the computer stores and jeans shops, is City Market. In one section are the imported rice and pastas. A charcuterie features such delights as quail and peppercorn pâtés, Italian salamis, double-smoked bacon, Texas barbeque, corned beef brisket and assorted sausages. The cheese counter offers brie, double and triple creams, chèvre and more. Prime meats, usually found only in restaurant kitchens, line the showcase of the meat section. In addition, a small but fashionable restaurant serves lunch and dinners; it also has a wine bar.

FOODSTUFFS
338 Park Avenue, Glencoe 60022. Telephone 835-5105. Hours: M–F 10–5:30, SAT 9–5. You can get on their free mailing list for seasonal and holiday specials by sending in your name and address.

There is no question that Foodstuffs is the best-stocked, most diversified and fun food store to visit on the North Shore. It is dedicated to the best of foods and ingredients, both for do-it-yourself cookery and ready made for carry-out. Not only is the stock of the highest quality, but sales people are able to field most questions about usage, storage and so forth. The pleasure of shopping at Foodstuffs includes just browsing through the aisles to see all the jams, jellies, fresh breads, tarts and cakes behind the counter, as well as the ready-to-go pâtés, terrines and mousses. In addition to major domestic and imported brands of specialty items, ranging from chutneys to coffees and teas, they also have some private-label commodities. If you want an unusual or exotic vinegar or perhaps a walnut oil you haven't been able to find elsewhere, or a cookie mold or pizzelle iron, chances are Foodstuffs will have what you need.

FOODWORKS
1002 West Diversey, Chicago 60614. Telephone 348-7800.
1527 West Morse Avenue, Chicago 60626. Telephone 465-6200.
937 West Armitage Avenue, Chicago 60614. Telephone 935-6800.
Hours: 9–8 daily. To be placed on mailing list, register at one of the stores.

Foodworks picks up where the ordinary supermarket leaves off. As in a supermarket, you will find all the basic staples and produce, but discriminating shoppers will also find much more in the way of foods and ingredients to meet individual tastes. The deli section, for example, features quality luncheon meats, sliced to order, many nitrate free. Freshly made salads and a selection of baked goods, tortes, cakes, and the like, are sold whole or by the piece. Several brands of natural foodstuffs plus a wide variety of imported and domestic cheeses are also stocked. Foodworks carries gourmet coffee beans in blends and bulk; customers can use the store's grinder, if they do not have one at home. And, there is an assortment of gourmet and specialty foods. A housewares section of the store displays Calphalon cookware, a variety of kitchen gadgets, mugs, soft goods and more.

HEL'S KITCHEN
1845 Second Street, Highland Park 60035. Telephone 433-1845. Hours: M–F 10–5:30, SAT 10–5, pickup orders only SUN 10–3.

While you have an interest in cooking (why else would you be looking at this book?), there are probably times when you simply do not have the time or energy to do the job yourself. In those times, it's good to know about stores such as Hel's Kitchen, a new family-owned carry-out. Everything they sell is made in the store, from their own blends of spices and fresh fruit vinegars to their breads, sauces, entrees and desserts. To assure freshness and variety, selections are changed seasonally to offer the best of what may be available in the marketplace. For example, summer entrees might feature such dishes as fresh Florida red snapper in papillote, boneless breast of chicken in phyllo, or herbed shrimp with basil-garlic mayonnaise. Fall selections might include duck jambalaya and "dirty" rice, or poached bass with white wine, fresh pears, shallots, mushrooms, leeks and tarragon. Hel's Kitchen also provides low-sodium, low-cholesterol dishes, as well as complete catering for small or large gatherings. The store offers an extensive listing of side dishes, sandwiches and desserts.

KENESSEY'S GOURMETS INTERNATIONALE

Hotel Belmont, 403 West Belmont Avenue, Chicago 60657. Telephone 929-7500. Hours: M–TH 11–11, F–SAT 11–12, SUN 12–9. Customers can register for the mailing list at the store.

Kenessey's combines a Viennese-style pastry shop on one floor with a separate wine shop, deli and gourmet specialty store on a second floor. The store stocks some 230 cheeses, sausages, hams and other meats from around the world. There are 1,500 different wines, most selected annually when proprietors Ivan and Kathy Kenessey go on their European buying spree. For beer drinkers, this is a paradise of more than a hundred different brands. For pastry lovers, Kenessey's staff bakes fresh each day scores of delicious Austro-Hungarian, French and other European pastries, cakes, pies, tortes, creams and the like. And, if you are confused by the wide selections of gourmet specialties, sales people will take the time to answer your questions. In addition to the takeout items, Kenessey's will also cater for small or large groups, and they serve lunch and dinner in the wine cellar seven days a week.

LABELLE GOURMET

16 West Calendar Court, La Grange 60525. Telephone 579-3300. Hours: M–SAT 9–6; December 6–30 SUN 12–4. Call or write for free subscription to monthly newsletter.

In the competitive field of gourmet specialties, LaBelle features a wide selection of freshly made products, as well as prepared delicacies from such major houses as Silver Palate, Conlon wine jellies and Judyth's Mountain sauces. They also bake daily their own croissants, cheesecakes, jumbo chocolate chip cookies and wedding cakes. For holidays such as Christmas, customers may order seasonal specials like bûche de Noël or croquembouche. Hot and cold hors d'oeuvres include seafood strudel, quiche and lasagna, not to mention fresh salads of broccoli, tarragon chicken and pasta primavera, to name a few. LaBelle also has a large, multipage gourmet catering menu with dozens of choices from appetizers through desserts.

MARSHALL FIELD & CO.

(Gourmet foods, wines, seventh floor.) 111 North State Street, Chicago 60602. Telephone 781-3668. Hours: T, W, F, SAT 9:45–5:45, M, TH 9:45–7.

The granddaddy of department store food shops, Field's range of products has yet to be duplicated in other department stores in town. Although prepared foods are mostly salads and pâtés, the spacious area is more than filled with imported condiments, coffees, teas, packaged foods and frozen items prepared in Field's kitchens. Recently, American-made condiments by such companies as the Silver Palate, Blanchard & Blanchard and Victorian Pantry have begun to outnumber the imports. Supplemented with a new wine cellar area and the famous bakery (home of the sinful Frango mint brownies), Field's can be a one-stop shopping trip for those too busy to cook.

METROPOLIS

163 West North Avenue, Chicago 60610. Telephone 642-2130. Hours: M–TH 11–9, F–SAT 11–10:30.

Old Town yuppies find this small gourmet takeout shop and cafe the perfect solution to busy-day dinners—at reasonable prices. All the food is made on the premises, and the menu changes daily with offerings such as calzone, lasagna, seafood strudels, ginger crêpes with wild mushrooms and goat cheese, excellent stuffed roasted Cornish hens, and intriguing wild rice jambalaya. Some vegetarian sandwiches and entrees are also available. Desserts may be a delectable fig tart, flourless chocolate cake or house-made gelato in intriguing flavors such as kiwi.

MITCHEL COBEY CUISINE
100 East Walton, Chicago 60611. Telephone 944-3411. Hours: M–F 10–6:30, SAT 10–6.

If you're seeking a caterer to the stars, look no further than Mitchell Cobey, who has done parties for the likes of Katharine Hepburn and Helen Hayes. Cobey will do the whole job for you, or you can select individual items and build a menu on your own. For example, consider his mouthwatering selection of hors d'oeuvres—salmon tartar wrapped in thin slices of smoked salmon, or small new potatoes filled with caviar and crème fraîche, or escargots in profiteroles with pernod sauce. The list goes on and on. Most of the food is made by Cobey and his associates, including such specialty products as pâtés, candies, salads and pastries. He also stocks a large variety of cheeses. Some of the more unusual goat cheeses in a selection of about twenty include taupinère, a creamy cheese covered in paprika, herbs or pepper; selle fur cher, a small, round, medium-strong cheese with a mold rind; and couer chèvre, a heart-shaped cheese rolled in ash. The shop also carries a full line of French cheese, including excellent brie. The retail store opened in 1977, after Cobey did his apprenticeship as a private caterer. Located in the heart of Chicago's classiest neighborhood, his foods reflect the epitome of good taste.

NEIMAN-MARCUS EPICURE SHOP
(Fourth floor), 737 North Michigan Avenue, Chicago 60611. Telephone 642-5900. Hours: M–TH 10–7, TU, W, F, SAT 10–6, SUN 12–5. The Epicure publishes a free mailing piece separate from the famous Neiman-Marcus catalog. You may sign in person or by phone. Also, ask to receive their free newsletter Cornucopia *which lists special events such as tastings, demonstrations and cooking classes.*

A visit to Neiman-Marcus' Epicure Shop is a culinary odyssey. They feature only the best. Yes, you will pay top dollar for that Petrossian caviar or smoked salmon foie gras, but their quality and authenticity are guaranteed. Epicure takes up some four thousand square feet of space on the fourth floor of Nieman's new Michigan Avenue store. Here, you will find a charcuterie, four bakery units and three refrigerated cases well stocked with salads, pastries, cheeses and even ready-made sauces. The bakery and chocolate bar will satisfy the sweet tooth that keeps fighting with your desire to count calories. Their chocolate truffle is a *trompe-l'oeil* version of the French fungi so prized by gourmands; these truffles, however, are filled with creamy dark chocolate mixed with various liqueurs and nut extract flavorings. For do-it-yourselfers, Epicure has a wide selection of ingredients for the creative cook. The Neiman-Marcus stores in Oak Brook and Northbrook Court have limited selections of specialty foods, but not the fresh food department that distinguishes the downtown location.

PANICO'S TASTEBUDS
Suite 150, Port Clinton Square, Highland Park 60035. Telephone 433-7034.
Hours: M–SAT 10:30–6:30, TH until 7.

Chef Andrew Panico has cooked rack of lamb for as many as two thousand diners for a catered event at Chicago's Shedd Aquarium. Now he brings this expertise to his shop in Highland Park's new Port Clinton Square. With recipes all in his head, Panico creates almost according to whim, from soups to salads to pastas. While specializing in carry-out Italian foodstuffs, he also provides French delights and occasionally other ethnic specialties. Panico's Tastebuds also offers full multi-course catering services.

TASTEBUDS
746 West Webster, Chicago 60614. Telephone 348-0333. Hours: TU–SAT 11–9,
SUN 11–8. Sign the guest book and get on their free mailing list for news of
future specials.

Even chef Louis Szathmary of the Bakery shops at Tastebuds, and if it's good enough for him . . . ! The two Chicago women who designed and own Tastebuds do all of the cooking, listing daily specials on a large blackboard. But you will always find such staples as fresh pasta salads, homemade basil pesto shells, fettuccine italiano with prosciutto and fresh grated parmesan, and even Oriental sesame noodles. There are also picnic baskets to go and fresh Italian sauces to carry out by the quart. An extensive catering department can whip up goodies for a small crowd or a few hundred of your nearest and dearest should you not feel up to the task yourself.

ZAMBRANA'S THE FOOD EMPORIUM
2346 North Clark Street, Chicago 60614. Telephone 935-0200. Hours: M–F
10–8, SAT 9–7, SUN 9–6.

One of Chicago's best gourmet shops in the variety of items sold, Zambrana's has a full range of prepared foods, cheeses, coffees, sausages, baked goods, pastas and sauces, and imported chocolates, all arranged attractively in a rather small space. Owner Manuel Zambrana has also brought in a small quantity of imported packaged items and wines to round out the selection. As you pick up your dinner party components, stop by the fresh-cut flower area to pick out your centerpiece. This Lincoln Park store is one of the most visually appealing and pleasant food shops in town.

Health Foods

Interest in health foods has grown beyond the diet and yoga set, to the point that almost every mainstream supermarket has a health food section these days. But, there are still those smaller, specialty shops that stock organically grown produce, naturally raised meats, and preservative-free packaged foods. Here is a representative sampling of health food stores in Chicago.

Also check listings under Spices & Herbs, Coffee & Tea and Dried Fruits & Nuts.

ALL THE BEST NUTRITION
3008 West Devon, Chicago 60659. Telephone 274-9478. Hours: M–W, F 10–6, TH 10–7, SAT 10–5, SUN 11–4. Sign up for catalog mailing list at store.
   Ask the owners of this five-year-old health food shop why they are in the business and you are likely to learn a lot about recovery from serious illness. Both claim to have conquered disease by proper diet. The store stocks organically grown grains, plus sugar-free and salt-free products. They even stock a brand of kosher vitamins! Prepared foods include vegetarian sandwiches and fresh vegetable juices.

BREAD SHOP
3400 North Halsted, Chicago 60657. Telephone 528-8108. Hours: M–SAT 9–8, SUN 11–5.
   Those looking for preservative-free whole-grain breads and baked goods come to the North Side's Bread Shop, a small storefront founded twelve years ago by a non-profit corporation. A wide variety of bread is baked on the premises daily, including a fine seven-grain whole wheat and an onion-dill bread. No granulated sugar or white flour is used. A nice touch: baking classes. The shop also carries an assortment of health foods on a few rows of dusty shelves.

FOODWORKS

1527 West Morse Avenue, Chicago 60626. Telephone 465-6200.
1002 West Diversey Avenue, Chicago 60614. Telephone 348-7800.
937 West Armitage Avenue, Chicago 60614. Telephone 935-6800.
Hours: 9–8 daily.

The owners of Foodworks have expanded on the concept of the typical health food store and in the process have made shopping fun in their three shops. The Diversey Avenue store is more like a large supermarket with a touch of gourmet. The produce, for example, is not organically grown, but it is beautiful and well selected for size and quality. In addition to produce, the store carries meat, cheeses and prepared foods—a one-stop food market. The concept must be working: A third, although slightly smaller, store on Armitage Avenue has just opened. The Morse Avenue location is much smaller and lacks a meat department. All of the shops use attractive displays to sell items. Whole grains, natural potato chips and seaweeds can be found. Some natural cosmetics and vitamins are carried. The "naturally raised" chicken at the Diversey store is excellent.

RAINBOW GROCERY

946 West Wellington Avenue, Chicago 60614. Telephone 929-1400. Hours: M–F 9–6, SAT 8–4.

Tucked under the El tracks down the street from the huge Illinois Masonic Hospital complex, this is one of Chicago's first quality cooperative health food shops. It is tiny, but attractively arranged, and fun to browse in. For a fee, members get a 10 percent discount on foods. Some of the produce is organically grown. Rainbow also stocks frozen prepared health foods and a wide selection of whole grains, beans and nuts in attractive bins as well as the usual array of packaged products. The cooperative is run by the owners of the Foodworks chain.

Meats

It's not for nothing that Carl Sandburg labeled Chicago "Butcher for the world." While our famous stockyards have disappeared, Chicago is still a meat town where quality is as important as quantity. While our Jewel, Dominick's and other supermarket chains offer high-quality meats, it is the neighborhood butcher, often German, Hungarian or Italian, who feeds us like kings. We are pampered by aproned men serving up thick sirloins, prime porterhouses, pork loins and hams.

But above all we're spoiled by an array of sausages that won't quit, often made by men with accents as thick and sturdy as their products: bratwurst, cervelat, cotechino, metwurst, kielbasa, bangors, black puddings and more.

When we refer to prime or choice meats, we are referring to the USDA grades.

Many sources for meat are also found in the Ethnic Foods chapter: Specifically, visit Kuhn's and Meyer Imports for German sausages, while Italian markets such as Riviera, Gino's and Joseph Food Mart have extensive selections of salamis, bologna and butchered meats. Among the stores in the Gourmet & Takeout Foods chapter, good butcher shops are found at City Market, Foodworks, Kenessey's and Zambrana's. Check, too, Randolph Street Market in the Produce chapter. For game meats, see Czimer's and Wild Game, Inc. in Poultry & Game.

BARNEY'S MEAT MARKET
1648 East 55th Street, Chicago 60615. Telephone 752-0146. Hours: M–SAT 9–6.

At Barney's all meats are handcut; you won't find a power saw in the place. Customers may phone in their orders and come in later to pick them up without having to wait. This is basically a neighborhood market for Chicago's Hyde Park area, as it has been since 1927, with some pretty illustrious customers—University of Chicago presidents and Nobel Prize winner Saul Bellow among them. The market hangs sides of beef, choice and prime, and makes custom cuts for customers. Only grade A poultry is sold, and it's ice packed only, never frozen.

BORNHOFEN'S MEAT MARKET
1122 Thorndale Avenue, Chicago 60660. Telephone 561-1484. Hours: M–SAT 9–6.

Bornhofen's has been in business since 1910, serving the North Sheridan Road area near the lake with a full line of quality, prime-grade meats, fresh poultry and homemade Italian and German sausages. The service is friendly and professional.

CITY MEAT MARKET
27 West Jefferson Street, Naperville 60540. Telephone 355-0440. Hours: M–SAT 8:30–6.

Here is a real find, as far away from the typical supermarket meat department as a butcher can be and still be in the fresh meat business. The sawdust on the floor is as real as the genuine desire to please customers and meet their needs. The shop has been in business since the 1890s. The present owners have had it since 1971 and cheapness is not their goal. "You get what you pay for!," is the guiding philosophy at City Meat Market. In addition to finding aged steaks, pork roasts, boneless leg of lamb and other specialty products, customers can purchase such brand-name products as those from Slotkowski and Hoka. Custom orders are handled routinely without difficulty. So, if you need a particular kind of smoked butt, or a veal pocket stuffed with duxelles, this is the place to shop. If you don't live in or near Naperville, one visit and you'll wish you had City Meat Market close to home.

CONTINENTAL MEAT MARKET
3922 North Lincoln Avenue, Chicago 60613. Telephone 549-7240. Hours: M–F 7–6, SAT 9–4.

Located in an old German neighborhood, this clean shop deals in made-on-the-premises bologna, liver sausage, bratwurst and other German sausages. Smoked hams and pork and a good selection of fresh meats also are offered.

E & M PROVISIONS
3358 Dempster Road, Skokie 60076. Telephone 679-6950. Hours: M–T, TH–F 8–5, W, SAT 8–2.

ELEGANCE IN MEATS
3135 Dundee Road, Northbrook 60052. Telephone 480-6328. Hours: M–F 9–6, SAT 9–5, SUN 10–4.

At the Skokie location, you'll find an old-fashioned, full-service butcher shop run by the Manacek family and offering prime and choice meats as well as poultry and seafood. Everything here looks great and is great. The Manaceks recently expanded to the second location in Northbrook and added lines of deli items, prepared gourmet foods and baked goods.

EBNER'S KOSHER MEAT MARKET
2649 West Devon Avenue, Chicago 60659. Telephone 743-8244 or 764-1446. Hours M–TH 7–6, F 7–1.

Ebner's specializes in prime beef and poultry in a tiny shop on bustling Devon Avenue where it has been in business for eighteen years.

GEPPERTH'S MARKET
1970 North Halsted Street, Chicago 60614. Telephone 549-3883. Hours: M–SAT 9–5.

The Gepperth family bought this North Side butcher shop back in 1917 and earned a city-wide reputation for high-quality meats and personalized service. About four years ago, the family sold part of the business to Otto Demke and Harry Biebelmann who have continued the top-notch service and a small but excellent array of meats and poultry, as well as a small line of grocery products. The old storefront shop is nothing much to look at, but customers from the affluent Lincoln Park neighborhood flock in for the prime meats, homemade German sausages and smoked hams. Fresh turkeys can be ordered for holiday feasts.

HONEY BAKED HAM COMPANY
8615 South Stoney Island Avenue, Chicago 60617. 734-6700.
3018 West Belmont Avenue, Chicago 60618. Telephone 588-4327.
Hours: TU–SAT 9–6.

The perfect solution for parties, showers, receptions and summer picnics for crowds, a honey-baked ham has a wonderful sweet-cured flavor and a lean texture that's hard to duplicate at home. It's worth the $3.50 a pound to pick one up, already sliced, if you wish.

JOE'S HOMEMADE SAUSAGE
4452 North Western Avenue, Chicago 60625. Telephone 478-5443. Hours: M–F 9–6, SAT 9–4.

Over thirty-six kinds of sausages make this North Side shop a sausage-lover's paradise. The shop has been in this location for twenty years and now is owned by a Yugoslavian, so you'll find plenty of sausages in the style of that country as well as Hungary, Poland, Germany and other Eastern European countries. A selection of cheeses is available. Expect friendly service and a real neighborhood feel.

KOSHER ZION MEATS
5529 North Kedzie Avenue, Chicago 60625. Telephone 463-3351. Hours: M–W 8–4:30, TH 8–5, SAT 8–3:30.

Probably most famous for its kosher hot dogs which are sold at Wrigley Field, this small sausage factory also churns out excellent salami, Romanian pastrami and other sausages. A line of kosher meats and poultry is sold as well as prepared on-the-premises frozen meat entrees such as chicken Kiev. Friendly service helps make the trip to this North Side market worthwhile.

MIKOLAJCZYK SAUSAGE SHOP
1737 West Division Street, Chicago 60622. Telephone 486-8870. Hours: M–SAT 8–6.

Over fifty years ago, this small butcher shop began selling Polish specialty sausages and still does so today even though most of the Polish immigrants to Chicago have moved on to other locations beyond this near West Side neighborhood. The shop is noted for its fine liver sausages, salami, Polish hams and bacon. You don't need to speak Polish to get fine, friendly service.

MILLSTEIN KOSHER MEAT MARKET
2604 West Devon Avenue, Chicago 60659. Telephone 262-9617 or 274-0430. Hours M–TH 6:30–5, F 6:30–noon.

Since 1936, this Devon Avenue shop has been catering to this Jewish neighborhood on Chicago's North Side with a good selection of strictly kosher beef, lamb and poultry.

OLD WILLOW MARKET
2710 Old Willow Road, Northbrook 60062. Telephone 724-8930. Hours: M–F 8:30–5:30, SAT 8:30–5.

In seven years of business, the Old Willow Market may have grown bigger, but it still has a personal touch with customers. Homemade Italian and Polish sausages are the specialties. The shop is also a great source for prime beef and Provimi veal when only perfection will do. In short, the store offers quality in its wares and excellent service that includes free delivery.

PAULINA MARKET
3501 North Lincoln Avenue, Chicago 60657. Telephone 248-6272. Hours: M–F 9–6, SAT 9–5.

This old-time German neighborhood meat market has moved recently to spiffy new and larger quarters up the street. But you can still buy high-quality German-style sausages and a full line of choice and prime meats there. Specialties are any of the homemade sausages, including delicate German bratwurst, frankfurters and a fine, spicy Hungarian salami that's redolent with paprika. Plump, dressed poultry is also offered. Hanging on the back wall are assorted sizes of whole Virginia country hams and dried sausages. Service here is friendly and speedy, unless the usual Saturday morning crowd grows too quickly.

PFAELZER BROTHERS
4501 West District Boulevard, Chicago 60632. Telephone 325-9700. Mail-order only.

This old-time West Side Chicago firm specializes in national mail-order frozen prime beef. Great for gift giving. A catalog is available by writing to the company.

ROMANIAN KOSHER SAUSAGE COMPANY
7200 North Clark Street, Chicago 60626. Telephone 561-4141. Hours: M–TH 9–6, F 8–3:15, SUN 9–5.

For seventeen years, this far North Side wholesale and retail firm has made a name with its deli items such as smoked turkey, franks and salami, as well as its full line of choice and prime meats and poultry. Pick up a dry salami and some bread for a picnic in the park just across the street.

VIENNA SAUSAGE MANUFACTURING COMPANY
2501 North Damen Avenue, Chicago 60647. Telephone 235-6652. Hours: M–F 9–5, SAT 9–3:45.

Vienna hot dogs are as well known in Chicago as Coney Island dogs are in New York. They are sold all over Chicago, but the retail store at the factory gives hot-dog lovers a break of a dollar or more per pound on slightly imperfect franks. Also available at regular retail prices are top-of-the-line natural casings, luncheon meats, Polish sausages, corned beef, potato salad and cole slaw.

WINSTON SAUSAGES
4701 West 63rd Street, Chicago 60629. Telephone 767-4353 or 284-9245. Hours: M–SAT 9–6.

Specializing in Irish, Scottish and English sausages, this tidy shop near Midway Airport also carries British preserves, shortbreads and some baked goods such as Irish soda bread and Scottish black buns, which are similar to dark fruitcakes. English bangors, black puddings, meat pies and Irish country sausages are made on premises. Owner Mike Winston also offers Polish, Italian and Cajun sausages, plus a full line of meats.

Wholesale Meats

In the Randolph Street Market area, shoppers will find small butcher shops that cater to wholesale amounts, though retail customers are welcome. Look for bargains in pork cuts and lamb. Many of the butchers are Greek, so lamb is often featured.

COLUMBUS MEAT MARKET
906 West Randolph Street, Chicago 60607. Telephone 829-2480. Hours: M–SAT 7–5, SUN 8–1.

G & J MEAT PACKING COMPANY
916 West Randolph Street, Chicago 60607. Telephone 226-8633. Hours: M–SAT 8–4:30.

OLD MARKET MEATS
842 West Randolph Street, Chicago 60607. Telephone 421-6446. Hours: M–SAT 8–5, SUN 9–noon.

OLYMPIC MEAT PACKERS
810 West Randolph Street, Chicago 60607. Telephone 666-2222. Hours: M–SAT 7:30–5:30, SUN 9–noon.

Poultry & Game

Shoppers today seem more aware of the quality of poultry available to them than at any other time. The recent popularity of free-range chicken and a wider variety of game listed on restaurant menus have helped educate the consumer. Although today's supermarket chickens are one of the most economical protein buys in the marketplace, many shoppers are looking for birds with more flavor that also have been raised without additives in their feed. As for turkey, more and more supermarkets are offering fresh as well as the standard frozen holiday birds.

It is difficult to find free-range chicken in Chicago. The term itself has not been clearly defined. Does it mean, for example, that the bird has been fed additive-free grains? Or has it simply been free to roam around the farmyard? Some stores, such as Foodworks (listed under Health Foods), use the term "naturally raised" for their chicken. Until more strict labeling is required, it's best to use caution when you see a free-range label.

The following are just a few of the fine poultry sources in the area. Also check the chapter on Meats; many of the butchers listed there also carry poultry. Ethnic shops, health food stores, and gourmet food stores with meat sections are other sources.

CZIMER'S WILD GAME MARKET
159th Street (Route 7, 4½ miles east of LaGrange Road), Lockport 60441.
Telephone 460-2210. Hours: M–SAT 9–5. Call or write to be included on their
mailing list.

"Right now, we're out of hippopotamus, but I can get some for you," said one
of the five Czimer brothers rather apologetically when we inquired about just how
wild their wild game is. But, routinely you can find anything from alligator or
eland to zebra, plus the more commonly eaten deer and bison, as well as game
birds including ptarmigan, quail, wild turkey or mallard duck. Czimer's has been
in business since 1914, originally as a fresh meat market with only occasional
game in season. After World War II, when the senior Czimer's sons went into business with their father, one brother developed an interest in raising pheasants. Thus
started the broad array that now makes Czimer's nationally known as a retailer and
wholesale shipper of wild foods. Some meats come in from Lapland, including
deer, elk and moose. Africa supplies more exotic fare such as lion meat and the
occasional giraffe. The store features a full stock of condiments and seasonings to
complement a big game dinner. By the way, those llamas or spotted fallow deer
you'll see roaming around in the large fenced side yard won't find their way onto a
dinner table. They're kept as pets to amuse children and others attracted to Czimer's mini-zoo.

DIANA FARMS
3232 South Halsted Street, Chicago 60608. Telephone 326-6966. Hours: TU–F
9–6, SAT 9–5.

This tidy shop has been serving the Bridgeport neighborhood on the South Side
for years with fresh dressed chickens, capons and turkeys.

GEORGIA FARMS
2120 Central Street, Evanston 60201. Telephone 864-4887. Hours: M–F 9–5:30, SAT 9–5.

This twenty-five-year-old business has grown from a simple poultry shop to a multiproduct operation that offers fresh and frozen wild game, buffalo, turkey, chicken, quail, poussin and ribs, as well as cheeses and prepared salads. The cheeses are all from Wisconsin and include Swiss, blue cheese, brie and aged cheddar. Smoked and barbecued poultry make a fine takeout meal.

HARRISON POULTRY
1220 Waukegan Road, Glenview 60015. Telephone 724-0132. Hours: M–SAT 8–6.

The store has been remodeled considerably over the decades and it is no longer owned by the founding family, but Harrison Poultry has occupied the same location for nearly ninety years. Although they do not slaughter on the premises as in years gone by, they do buy fresh farm-slaughtered birds, including squabs, pheasants and Long Island ducklings, as well as the more commonplace chicken, turkey and goose. The store also carries some frozen ready-to-cook cuts and pieces, fresh eggs, sauces, condiments and poultry seasonings.

JOHN'S LIVE POULTRY AND EGG MARKET
5955 West Fullerton Avenue, Chicago 60639. Telephone 622-2813. Hours: TU–W 9–4, TH–SAT 8–6.

Buying a live chicken is one way to ensure freshness. Although you may feel a bit uncomfortable selecting a live chicken, knowing its fate, and although the price is higher than any supermarket chicken, you will be well rewarded by the flavor. John's also deals in game birds, such as pheasant and quail, fresh in season or frozen out of season. His chickens are raised by Amish farmers in Indiana who use no chemical additives in the grain feed given to the birds. White and brown chicken eggs are available, as well as more exotic goose, duck and quail eggs. The small shop has been under the same ownership for twenty-five years.

SCHAUL'S POULTRY & MEAT COMPANY
7221 North Harlem Avenue, Niles 60648. Telephone 647-9304. Hours: M–F 9–6, SAT 9–5:30. A mail-order gift catalog is available.

Schaul's has specialized in fresh turkey since 1923, when the current owner's grandfather started the business selling turkeys out of his home. Now the company promotes its fresh capons, chicken and ducks, as well as turkey and a full line of prime beef. A line of gourmet foods and hors d'oeuvre under the Schaul's label is also sold.

WILD GAME, INC.

*1941 West Division Street, Chicago 60622. Telephone 278-1661; 24-hour
answering machine.*
868 North Orleans Street, Chicago 60610. Telephone 944-0882.
Hours: M–F 9–6. Catalog available.

Kaye Zubow began providing wild game to Chicago restaurants over three years
ago to fill an obvious need. Little wild game was readily available unless it was
frozen. Today Zubow has taken on two partners, added a new retail shop and an
office in Dallas and expanded the client list to include well-known local restaurants
such as Le Français and Ambria, while out-of-town customers include the United
Nations. Fresh Pekin (Long Island) duck, pheasant, squab, poussin, quail, moul-
lard ducks and partridge are offered now at retail and for mail order nationwide.
Wild Game has even managed to air freight in fine wild venison from New Zealand, sometimes frozen, sometimes fresh. Recently the firm also added to its product list wild American and French mushrooms, American cheeses and truffles. For
Thanksgiving and other holidays, it offers wild turkey, goose and smoked turkey
and pheasant. Also from New Zealand are the prized, green-lipped mussels. Gift
collections of game can be shipped in wooden crates.

Produce

A dedicated coterie of gourmands in Chicago will regularly get up in the middle of the night to be first at the Randolph Street Market produce dealers. While many dealers are wholesalers, a number will sell to retail customers, if the volume makes it worthwhile. But, for those of us who may buy only a small bag of radishes or a few heads of lettuce, the produce counter at the neighborhood supermarket may be adequate or we may choose one of the specialty produce stores which dot the city. But look for a store with enough turnover of product to ensure freshness; beware of shops that show wilted greens or soft fruits. Don't be afraid to feel and smell a cabbage or citrus. Maybe you can't squeeze the Charmin, but don't ever buy a melon without testing it first with a little squeeze and a knock or two on the rind.

There are more greengrocers out there than you might imagine. Some are here today, gone tomorrow, as the saying goes. But even though freshness may be fleeting, quality endures. Look for those shops that have been neighborhood fixtures for some time. If you want a specialty green, perhaps maché or radicchio, ask that it be stocked. And, if you have doubts about how to store or use a particular product, again ask. If you don't get an answer, that's a good sign to shop elsewhere. The quality greengrocer not only sells, he gives advice and knowledge.

Many of the gourmet and takeout food shops in Chicago have selections of more exotic produce such as blood oranges, starfruit, lychee nuts. Also, look under Ethnic Foods and Health Foods and check Herbs Now in the chapter on Spices & Herbs.

CAPUTO'S FOOD MARKET
2558 North Harlem Avenue, Elmwood Park 60635. Telephone 453-0155. Hours: M–F 5 a.m.–9 p.m., SAT 5–8, SUN 5–9.

Some great prices can be found in this Italian neighborhood market where the wet floors and open garage-like doorways remind one of an old-time farmers market. Blood oranges, cactus pears, fresh fennel and escarole are found among the huge piles of apples, potatoes, greens and broccoli. A small selection of pasta, Italian bread, oils and dried sausages round out the inventory.

THE CARROT TOP
1430 Paddock Drive, Northbrook 60062. Telephone 279-1450. Hours: M–SAT 9–6.

This popular indoor produce market may be somewhat hard to find (it's off Willow Road), but people who flock here swear by the quality of greens and other vegetables and fruits. All produce is displayed in boxes, just as they might be at a farmers' market, and the store is redolent with earthy aromas. Carrot Top is particularly favored as a source for hard-to-locate items such as arugula, radicchio and shiitake mushrooms. They also have an excellent selection of fresh herbs and Oriental vegetables. Although they stock a variety of other items such as jams and bulk nuts, cheeses, muffins, breads and homemade-style cookies, this is not a full-line marketplace.

NORTHEASTERN FRUIT AND GARDEN MARKET
6000 North Lincoln Avenue, Chicago 60659. Telephone 338-0610. Hours: M–SAT 8:30–7:30, SUN 9–8.

A family-owned-and-run business since 1908, Northeastern Fruit is not located in the northeastern part of Chicago, but rather at a far northwestern intersection. Who knows why, but the nice displays of fresh produce soon take your mind off the question. In addition to the usual favorites, you can find persimmons, mangoes and kiwis in season, and Belgian endive, imported French shallots, fresh coriander, cactus pears, plantains, chilies and bok choy.

OLD WORLD MARKET
5129 North Western Avenue, Chicago 60640. Telephone 989-4440. Hours: 7–10 daily.

This spacious wholesale and retail produce market carries nice-looking fruits and vegetables, augmented by Oriental and Latin specialties and some packaged products. You'll find nuts in bulk, dried and fresh chilies, tamarind, Thai eggplant and some frozen fish and baccalà (salted and dried cod). Reasonable prices.

ROGERS PARK FRUIT MARKET
7401 North Clark Street, Chicago 60626. Telephone 262-3663. Hours: M–SAT 8:30–9, SUN 9–6.

A good mix of produce answers the needs of this ethnically mixed far-north neighborhood. Between the oranges and apples you'll find tomatillos, guavas, papayas, boniatos, daikons and dried and fresh chilies as well as nuts, bread and some canned juices. Reasonable prices.

TREASURE ISLAND
Main office: 3460 North Broadway Avenue, Chicago 60657. Telephone 327-4265. Hours: M–F 8–9, SAT 8:30–9, SUN 8:30–6.

This eight-store supermarket chain bills itself as a "European-style" shopping experience. Produce, for example, is not hygenically wrapped in plastic on trays, but is naked and ready to be turned and pinched by smart shoppers. Then the items are weighed and priced right in the produce department by a generally helpful and knowledgeable staff. That alone makes it fun to shop at T. I. But when you add the wide variety and great-looking fruits and vegetables, you've just clinched the deal.

WHEATON MUSHROOM FARM
23 West 636 St. Charles Road, Wheaton 60188. Telephone 668-5709. Hours: M–F, 8–4, SAT 8–3.

Looking for fresh mushrooms and don't want to head for the forest? This family-run, twenty-seven-year-old farm may be the solution. Button mushrooms that, like all commercially raised mushrooms, are grown in the dark come in small, medium or large sizes at $1.50 a pound, a price hard to beat in the supermarket. The farm also sells compost in case you want to try a little growing of your own, whether it be mushrooms or garden veggies.

fine Oranges fine Lemons.

Wholesale Produce

Chicago has two main wholesale produce markets: South Water Market and the Randolph Street Market. At South Water, they don't want to be bothered with small purchases and the produce is often hidden away in the grungy warehouses. You must buy by the case and have a resale tax number, as do the owners of restaurants and food markets. But if you have a food co-op or a large group that wants to buy together, it may be worth investigating.

RANDOLPH STREET MARKET

Randolph in recent years has begun catering to retail customers and so it is much easier to shop there. The area is also closer to everyone's image of a wholesale market, with stacks of fresh watermelons, tomatoes, peaches and lettuces in season lining the street in front of each warehouse.

Located just west of the Loop on Randolph Street between Halsted on the east and Racine on the west, this old market area seems to be making an interesting comeback. While wholesale food businesses are located on the first floors of the warehouses, artists and entrepreneurs are taking over the large lofts in the top floors. If the trend continues, it looks like good news for this rather desolate district.

For the best selection the time to shop Randolph Street is early morning. Be prepared to face brusque salespeople and to buy in case lots in some firms. At noon it's fun to visit a couple of down-to-earth restaurants where you can hobnob with the produce men. Fish, meat and grocery goods are also sold along Randolph Street. Here are a few of the more accessible dealers.

GREEN GARDEN PRODUCE
942 West Randolph Street, Chicago 60607. Telephone 733-5054 or 733-5539.
Hours: M–F 4 am–3 pm, SAT 5 am–1 pm.
Fresh and frozen produce is offered by the case only here. Okra and dill were recently spotted, in addition to regular items of lettuce, tomatoes and other basic vegetables.

N. KANARIS PRODUCE COMPANY
806–808 West Randolph Street, Chicago 60607. Telephone 733-5595. Hours:
5 am–7 pm daily.
In season crates of watermelons line the sidewalk in front of this friendly dealer who specializes in wholesale and retail amounts of fresh produce.

D. J. KAROS COMPANY
832 West Randolph Street, Chicago 60607. Telephone 829-9788 or 226-6776.
Hours: M–SAT 5 am–3 pm.
Wide range of produce and a friendly staff, including one salesman who quipped: "We have everything here, except brains."

N & G PRODUCE
902–904 West Randolph Street, Chicago 60607. Telephone 942-9432. Hours:
M–SAT 6 am–5:30 pm, SUN 6 am–3 pm.
Easily the most attractive setup in the market, the produce looks good enough to take home and photograph. Prices are scribbled on a giant blackboard and a wide range of items includes baby artichokes, Japanese eggplants, tomatillos, Belgian endive and fresh herbs.

TED SAXRAS PRODUCE
900 West Randolph Street, Chicago 60607. Telephone 243-6570. Hours: M–SAT
5:30 am–6 pm, SUN 7–3.
Very nice looking produce is sold in wholesale and retail amounts here. As many as six kinds of chili peppers are often available.

Farmers Markets

It took Chicago a while to catch onto the farmers market bandwagon. But the city has made up for the slow start by allowing eight farmers markets to flourish from July through October each year. The markets are set up in neighborhood parking lots where growers from Michigan, Illinois and Indiana park their trucks filled with produce, honey, flowers, juices and preserves. While surveys have found that the prices at farmers markets may not save shoppers much money, the produce is often fresher than that found in supermarkets. Besides, the open-air shopping is so much more fun.

Farmers markets are also found in many suburbs. Call a specific town's chamber of commerce or city hall to determine if it sponsors a market there.

IN CHICAGO

The following markets are open from 7 am to 2 pm late June through October. For exact dates, call the City of Chicago Department of Consumer Services, 744-4006.

AUSTIN, Central Avenue and Madison street, Saturdays.

BACK OF THE YARDS, 47th and Justine streets, Thursdays.

DOWNTOWN, Daley Civic Center Plaza, Washington and Dearborn streets on selected dates only.

LINCOLN PARK, Armitage Avenue and Halsted street, Saturdays.

LINCOLN SQUARE, Lawrence and Oakley avenues, Tuesdays.

MORGAN PARK-BEVERLY, 95th and Vanderpoel streets, Saturdays.

NEAR SOUTH, 29th Street and Martin Luther King Drive, Saturdays.

SIX CORNERS, Irving Park and Clover streets, Wednesdays.

IN THE SUBURBS

AURORA, Water Street Mall, 7:30–noon, Saturdays.

DES PLAINES, Lee and Perry streets, 8–1, Saturdays.

ELMHURST, Addison Avenue between First and Second streets, 7–1:30, Wednesdays.

EVANSTON, Maple Avenue between Clark and Emerson streets, 8–3, Saturdays.

FOREST PARK, 7246 West Harrison street, 8–2 Saturdays.

HIGHLAND PARK, Roger Williams Avenue, between St. Johns and Dean avenues, Wednesdays.

HINSDALE, Garfield Avenue, one block south of Burlington Northern station, 8–2, Mondays.

HOMEWOOD, 18700 block of Dixie Highway, 8–2, Saturdays.

NORTHFIELD, Happ Road, next to Northfield Bowling Alley, 8–2, Saturdays.

OAK PARK, Lake Street and Elmwood Avenue, 8–2, Saturdays.

SKOKIE, 5127 Oakton Street, 8–2, Sundays.

WHEATON, Main Street and Liberty Drive, 8–2, Thursdays.

Spices & Herbs

Every schoolchild knows that Christopher Columbus was seeking a new route to the Orient so the Spanish could find new ways to bring in the spices and herbs they craved. Just think how bland our cooking would be without those countless seasonings we now take for granted. Spice and herb shops are among the most interesting stores for browsing—a pleasure that's intensified by the heavy and complex aromas from the myriad fragrances that lie in storage. But soon you will distinguish the fresh sharpness of nutmeg from the pungent sweetness of basil. Simon and Garfunkle may have reminded us of the loveliness of "Parsley, Sage, Rosemary and Thyme," but that is only a small sampling of an herbal bouquet.

When purchasing dried spices and herbs, buy in the smallest quantity convenient to your needs. Store in dim light or darkness inside tightly sealed containers. All herbs and spices have relatively short shelf lives, and in fact no two batches are likely to have the same potency. That's why measurements in a given recipe must be used only as a starting point. It is axiomatic that seasoning is a matter of taste, whether one is using a ground chili powder for a hearty Tex-Mex recipe, or a dash of oregano to finish a marinara sauce.

Fresh herbs can be frozen for use out of season. Be sure they are properly sealed to protect against freezer burn. Or, for something more unusual, soak fresh herbs in good olive oil and store refrigerated. You'll get a nicely flavored oil out of the bargain. Discard the leaves when you use the oil, after they have marinated for a few days.

For other sources of herbs and spices, see the Coffee and Tea Exchange (in the chapter on Coffee & Tea), Cuisine Unlimited (Cookware) and Nuts on Clark (Dried Fruits & Nuts). Also check the listings in Health Foods, Produce and Ethnic Foods, especially the Indian and Italian shops.

THE ETHNIC PANTRY
Box 798, Greyslake 60030. Telephone 223-6660. All orders may be made by telephone at any hour with credit card number or by mail order from their catalogs. To secure a catalog and be placed on their mailing list call or write. There is no charge.

The Ethnic Pantry is a real discovery. Their mail-order operation provides spices, herbs, specialty sauces and pastes for preparation of the cuisines of India, Indonesia and elsewhere in Southeast Asia. Spices and herbs are individually packaged in zippered plastic bags, so consumers can buy just the quantity needed. In fact, they recommend more frequent buying of smaller amounts rather than large purchases, since spices and the like do not always lend themselves to long-term storage. Customers can purchase spices individually or in so-called kits. For example, an Indian ingredient kit ($18.75) would include more than a dozen necessary spices or herbs with fenugreek, turmeric and whole green cardamom among them. A recent innovation is an Ethnic Pantry dinner pantry kit which provides a suggested menu with all recipes and complete serving suggestions, along with all spices and seasonings needed, plus specialty ingredients such as pappadams and basmati rice that you might not so easily find at a typical supermarket.

THE HERB SHOP
2557 North Halsted Street, Chicago 60614. Telephone 935-8343. Hours: M–SAT 12–6.

A tiny corner storefront, The Herb Shop offers over fifty varieties of fresh herbs in pots for you to take home and replant in your own garden or use immediately for cooking. Plenty of dried herbs and spices are also available, and there's a tiny deli counter with herb sauces such as the store's own pesto, one of the best in the city, and a pungent olive sauce made with green and black olives, parmesan cheese, garlic and herbs. Classes on cooking and gardening with herbs are also offered.

HERBS NOW
P.O. Box 775, Highland Park 60035. Telephone 432-7711. All business is done by mail or phone order. Call or write to be placed on the mailing list for catalogs and price lists.

Restaurant consultant David Brill has put together an interesting concept for the marketing of herbs, spices, produce and even unusual cheeses. He does it by mail order, making fresh products available to those who heretofore may have been limited to only the dried varieties. His catalogs and other mail material are mini-courses in the use and storage of herbs ranging from basil to tarragon and thyme. Although Herbs Now was originally set up to deal only with the restaurant and professional trade, it is possible for individual cooks and consumers to buy in small quantity. If it's cheese, perhaps an Alsatian munster or a Tome de Savoia, which you just cannot seem to find at the corner mini-mart, try Herbs Now. The inventory also includes fine charcuterie and pâtés. Hard-to-find produce, such as Spanish blood oranges, now can be found. Do you have have a recipe that requires sun-dried mushrooms or champagne vinegar? You've found the source.

THE SPICERY AND SAVORY SEASONINGS

227 Coffin Road, Long Grove 60047. Telephone 634-1616. Hours: M–F 10:30–5, SAT 11–5, SUN noon–6. Catalogs and brochures available by request.

Although The Spicery and Savory Seasonings has been open only since 1978, the look is of an old-fashioned country store, even down to the flounced aprons worn by the clerks, the bulk barrels and woodsy appointments. The Spicery is one of several shops that have grown up in the charming area of Long Grove. The store stocks bulk herbs, spice, coffees, teas and potpourris, with a sales volume that causes constant turnover, thus helping to ensure freshness. Most of the spices, herbs and the like can be brought in quantities as small as one ounce; of course, larger bulk purchases can be made, too. Wares include filé for Louisiana-style cookery, several kinds of bouquet garni, Chinese five spice powder and even a line of salt-free seasoning mixes. Some three dozen or more teas are regularly stocked as are more than a dozen varieties of coffee beans ready for fresh grinding. If you have no grinder, they will custom grind for drip, percolator and even espresso. The people who work at The Spicery obviously enjoy what they do. Sales people are cooks themselves, and are encouraged to take time with everyone, making you feel like the store's most important customer. It's a nice touch!

Wines

What can we say about wines in a few lines, when encyclopedias have been written on the subject? Just this: Look for a good wine merchant whom you can learn to trust. Taste, taste, taste. Read up on the subject. Learn what you can. Let your budget and your natural inclinations be your guide. And, above all follow one simple rule: *Enjoy!!!*

For Italian and German wines, check the listings in Ethnic Foods. Many of the stores in the Gourmet & Takeout Foods chapter also carry wine, such as Marshall Field and Kenessey's, which has some 1500 bottlings.

CHALET WINE & CHEESE SHOPS
405 West Armitage Avenue, Chicago 60614. Telephone 266-7155.
3000 North Clark Street, Chicago 60657. Telephone 935-9400.
40 East Delaware Street, Chicago 60610. Telephone 787-8555.
444 West Fullerton Parkway, Chicago 60614. Telephone 871-0300.
1525 East 53rd Street, Chicago 60615. Telephone 324-5000.
Hours vary from shop to shop.
Pleasant places to shop, the Chalet stores carry a good selection of wines from California and major wine-producing countries, plus imported beers. In the larger stores such as those on Delaware and Clark Street, you'll also find imported foods, prepared foods to go, coffee and tea and cheese. See cheese shops in the Dairy Products chapter for further description.

THE CELLARS
2820 North Sheffield Avenue, Chicago 60657. Telephone 880-0010. Hours: M–TH 10–9, F–SAT 10–10, SUN noon–6.

A small North Side wine shop with a limited though choice selection of wines, spirits and imported beers. The store's cellar is a tasting room plus storage for customers' private wine collections. Wine director Jim Steele has been credited with having the area's "best professional palate."

THE CHICAGO WINE COMPANY
5663 West Howard Street, Niles 60648. Telephone 647-8789; telex 206476. Hours: M–F 9–6, SAT 10–4. They send out six different types of mailings. A phone call or letter will get you on those that interest you.

The Chicago Wine Company claims to have the largest selection of wines available in the United States. Some ten years ago, wine lover John Hart had the proverbial dream of starting his own wine business, but with a difference. Hart wanted more than over-the-counter retail sales. He envisioned a large catalog, special search and procuring services for clients and a wine auction to rival the most famous; his latest auction catalog exceeds three hundred pages. Hart's Chicago Wine Company specializes in sales not only of the better-known and widely sought-after classified bottlings, but he searches out the smaller boutique wineries, too. If you're looking for a magnum, or even a larger bottle, of Chateau Pétrus, Romanée-Conti or the like, Hart's staff generally can find it for you. They will also appraise collections and consult on their sale to a direct buyer or through their auction.

FOREMOST LIQUORS
National headquarters, 5252 North Broadway Avenue, Chicago 60640. Telephone 334-0077. Hours vary.

With twenty-three stores in Chicago and twenty-nine in the suburbs, this is the area's biggest liquor chain. Foremost offers a liquor-by-wire service nationally.

CONNOISSEUR WINES, LTD.
77 West Chestnut (at Clark Street), Chicago 60610. Telephone 642-2375. Hours: TU–F 10–6, SAT 10–5. You will receive a free monthly catalog, if you request to be on their mailing list.

The address, 46 East Superior, may be more famous as the place where Hugh Hefner entered the publishing business, but in 1976 it became home to Chicago's Connoisseur Wines, Ltd. At first the shop was just a tasting room with table and chairs, but four years later, owner Pete Stern moved his business to larger quarters. The tasting room has been reproduced, but now an extensive inventory of hard-to-find imported wines is a major attraction for customers from all over the Midwest. Connoisseur Wines is probably best regarded as a source for difficult-to-find Bur-

gundies, both reds and whites, and some bottlings from the smaller shippers of the Rhône Valley. Stern's staff also regularly searches out inexpensive European wines of exceptional value.

ESSER'S WINES
405 Lake Cook Road, Lake Cook Plaza, Deerfield 60015. Telephone 272-2520. Hours: M–F 10–8, SAT 9–7, SUN 11–5. Customers may sign up to be placed on mailing list without cost.
2413 North Clark Street, Chicago 60614. Telephone 883-4440. Hours: M–F 11–9, SAT 10–7, SUN noon–5.

Esser's may be the most service-oriented wine shop around. They certainly try. The store holds regular classes and wine tastings, and usually several bottles are uncorked so you can taste particular specials or unusual items. You will find bottlings from the major and minor houses of France, Italy, Germany, California and other great wine-producing regions of the world. Wine lovers also will discover a full stock of wine literature and accessories. Not least of the attractions at Esser's is an in-house rating system. You may not agree with their likes and dislikes, but it's helpful to measure their guidelines against your personal tastes.

GOLD STANDARD LIQUORS
153 Skokie Valley Road, Highland Park 60035. Telephone 831-5400 (Chicago telephone 273-3625).
5100 Dempster Road, Skokie 60077. Telephone 674-4200.
6630 North Ridge Road, Chicago 60626. Telephone 465-3100.
3000 North Clark Street, Chicago 60657. Telephone 935-9400 or 975-7700. Hours vary from store to store.

Here's a liquor-store chain with a commitment to wine from around the world, including a good selection from California. Customers choose bottles from easy-to-identify bins. The stores also carry some imported packaged foods. The Clark Street store is teamed with a Chalet store and features packaged foods, cheeses and coffees.

LYNFRED WINERY
15 South Roselle Road, Roselle 60172. Telephone 529-WINE. Hours: 11–7 daily.

You would not expect to find an award-winning Chardonnay produced in Illinois. But that's exactly what has happened at Lynfred Winery. Its 1983 vintage received the best-of-show award from among 202 American Chardonnays tasted at the first annual National Restaurant Association competition in 1985. The winning bottling is now rather hard to come by, but Lynfred produces some three dozen other varietals, from Cabernet to Zinfandel, including some French hybrids such as Seyval Blanc and Vidal Blanc. The winery has no retail outlet beyond its own location, a large converted mansion with cellar walls eighteen inches thick. It's a treat to visit, tour and taste the wines. No, they don't grow their grapes here; Illinois cannot compete with the Napa Valley in that department. But they do get shipments from some of the better growers in and around Napa, as well as from other wine-growing areas throughout America.

SAM'S WINE WAREHOUSE
1000 West North Avenue, Chicago 60610. Telephone 664-4394. Hours: M–TH 7–9, F–SAT 7–10, SUN noon–6.

A Chicago institution. Wine lovers from out of state drive in with their station wagons to load up on Sam's deals (partly due to Illinois's reasonable liquor taxes and partly due to the low prices at Sam's). Recently Sam's moved down the street to a spic-and-span new location that some say isn't half the fun of the old, decrepit warehouse where yuppies fought with North Avenue bums for service. But Sam's bargains and wide selection remain the same. Look for unusual California boutique wines and a good selection of German and Alsatian bottlings.

SCHAEFER'S WINES
9965 Gross Point Road, Skokie 60076. Telephone 673-5711. Hours: M–SAT 9–9, SUN 11–5. The store publishes and distributes free of charge a catalog five times each year. Telephone or write to be included in future mailings.

Service is the name of the game in the wine business, and there is hardly a better place to shop in this area for wines than Schaefer's. Back in 1936, when George Schaefer, Sr., went into business, he opened a neighborhood tavern. That enterprise gave way to the wine store now owned and operated by his son George Schaefer, Jr., and there's hardly a question about wine that could not be answered by one of the salespeople. In addition to the extensive floor merchandise, Schaefer's maintains a temperature-controlled wine cellar which holds a huge collection of rare and boutique bottlings. The cellaring conditions are so ideal, in fact, that the wines to be sold at Christie's auctions in the United States are stored at Schaefer's for future delivery to winning bidders. Splendid tasting facilities include a private tasting room. And customers (or the just curious) can dial SAY-VINO (312-729-8466) for weekly telephone news updates about developments in the wine world, including vintage information and current Schaefer's specials.

A TASTE OF CALIFORNIA
340 West Armitage, Chicago 60614. Telephone 327-9465. Hours: M–F 9–5.

A Taste of California is a unique wine club, whose members receive top-quality premium California wines from many of the smaller, less well-known producers, as well as from the major-domos of the industry. Each month members are sent two bottles of the same varietal, but from different vineyards, with reds and whites alternated every other month. Members who choose to, can purchase these wines in six-bottle case lots at substantial discount. A newsletter features information about each month's selections. The club provides an intelligent and convenient way to sample selected California wines that ordinarily you might not be exposed to. Most selections average around $10 a bottle plus shipping and handling.

Wine & Beer Making Supplies

BREWIN' BEER
6037 West Irving Park Road, Chicago 60634. Telephone 685-2895. Hours: M, TH 10–8, TU–W, F–SAT 10–6.

All the equipment you need to brew beer, make wine, liqueurs and soda is sold here. Ingredients such as light and dark malts, hops and wine concentrates, plus complete recipes and instructions, will get any novice started. The owner was formerly a teacher of home brewing at a local college.

WINEMAKERS
689 West North Avenue, Elmhurst 60126. Telephone 834-0507. Hours: M–SAT 10–6. Coast-to-coast mail order.

Products and recipes are offered in this western suburban shop for making over one thousand wines and beers. In business fourteen years, the shop's owner concentrates on teaching techniques of classical winemaking. Free recipes and instructions. In addition to the usual wine and beer ingredients, the shop carries imported cordial extracts, wine racks, giftware and vinegar cultures.

Index

GEOGRAPHICAL INDEX

SUBJECT INDEX

CAROL HADDIX is food editor of the *Chicago Tribune* and formerly was food writer at the *Detroit Free Press*. She also edits restaurant reviews for the *Tribune*'s dining column and has contributed chapters on dining in Chicago and Detroit for *Where to Eat in America*.

SHERMAN KAPLAN has been reviewing the restaurants of Chicago for some seventeen years for WBBM-AM, the CBS radio station in Chicago, and is the author of the best-selling guidebook *Best Restaurants Chicago & Suburbs*. He also serves as an anchor man and reporter for WBBM.